What people are saying about

JESUS IN THE PRESENT TENSE

"In a day when many are offering cotton-candy theology, Warren Wiersbe takes us to the meat, bread, milk, and honey of the Word of God."

From the foreword by Michael Catt, senior
pastor of Sherwood Baptist Church, Albany, GA,
and executive producer of Sherwood Pictures

"Who Jesus Christ is really matters, now and for eternity. Warren Wiersbe brilliantly explores the great I AM—ness of Jesus. It's good to know who Christ is, but knowing what He can do for you is a matter of life and death, literally."

Palmer Chinchen, PhD, speaker and author
of *True Religion* and *God Can't Sleep*

What people are saying about …

WARREN W. WIERSBE

"Warren Wiersbe is one of the greatest Bible expositors of our generation."

Billy Graham, evangelist

"Dr. Wiersbe's unique style is not overly academic, but theologically sound. He explains the deep truths of Scripture in a way that everyone can understand and apply. Whether you're a Bible scholar or a brand-new believer in Christ, you will benefit, as I have, from Warren's insights."

Ken Baugh, pastor of Coast Hills
Community Church, Aliso Viejo, CA

JESUS
IN THE PRESENT TENSE

JESUS

IN THE PRESENT TENSE

The I AM *Statements of Christ*

WARREN W. WIERSBE

David C Cook®

transforming lives together

JESUS IN THE PRESENT TENSE
Published by David C Cook
4050 Lee Vance View
Colorado Springs, CO 80918 U.S.A.

David C Cook Distribution Canada
55 Woodslee Avenue, Paris, Ontario, Canada N3L 3E5

David C Cook U.K., Kingsway Communications
Eastbourne, East Sussex BN23 6NT, England

David C Cook and the graphic circle C logo
are registered trademarks of Cook Communications Ministries.

Bible credits appear on pages 193–194.

LCCN 2010939816
ISBN 978-0-7814-0487-7
eISBN 978-0-7814-0592-8

The Team: Don Pape, Karen Lee-Thorp, Sarah Schultz, Jack Campbell, Karen Athen
Cover Design: Amy Kiechlin
Cover Photo: iStockphoto

Printed in the United States of America
First Edition 2011

1 2 3 4 5 6 7 8 9 10

102910

CONTENTS

Foreword by Michael Catt

They say you judge a book by its cover. I've tried not to do that. Although I have nearly ten thousand books in my library, I seek to judge a book by the author and content. Covers can be misleading. Content is revealing.

As the author or editor of nearly two hundred books, Warren Wiersbe writes content that reveals a man who walks with God, listens to God, and knows God's Word intimately. The book you hold in your hands is no exception.

One of the first books I ever purchased as a young minister was one of Warren Wiersbe's "BE" series commentaries. That book helped me to stay balanced in my understanding of the Scriptures. As a pastor, I always check my Wiersbe commentaries to make sure I'm balanced on my interpretation of a text.

Warren Wiersbe is respected by Sunday school teachers and seminary professors. He is read by laymen and scholars. His insights have helped millions of students of God's Word.

In the 1990s, I finally got to meet Warren and his wife, Betty. Sometimes when you meet an author, you can see a vast difference between the person and the print. Not so with Warren. He lives what he writes. He loves the Lord he writes about. I am forever grateful for the opportunity to know him as a friend, encourager, and advisor. When I talk to him, I have pen and paper ready, because I know there's going to be a nugget of truth to write down and remember. I cherish every opportunity to talk … most of all, to listen.

This newest book from the desk of Dr. Wiersbe is what I would call "Classic Wiersbe." *Jesus in the Present Tense* is a journey through the I AM statements of our Lord (and a few other statements, as you will discover). These pages reveal the difference Christ makes today in the lives of those who embrace the truth. You will have a greater grasp of who Jesus *is* and what He wants to do in your life *today.*

Jesus in the Present Tense is a reminder that our Lord is not a distant deity, nor is He just a figure of history. He is the living God, the great I AM. Dr. Wiersbe guides us through a practical and applicable study of these statements. While these statements are familiar, we often forget they are for us today, not just for those who heard them in the first century.

When you read this book, you'll love Jesus more. You'll see how the divine life is intended to work itself out in daily living. Many books today seek to water down truth to make it more acceptable, but not this one. This book will stretch you to look to the Lord daily for all your needs.

In a day when many are offering cotton-candy theology, Warren Wiersbe takes us to the meat, bread, milk, and honey of the Word of God. The content is sound and scriptural. May the I AM speak to you, as He did to me.

Michael Catt
Senior pastor of Sherwood Baptist Church, Albany, Georgia
Executive producer of Sherwood Pictures

PREFACE

There is no substitute for Jesus Christ. Only Jesus can save us from our sins and give us the grace we need to live for Him. If you want fullness of life, you have to go to Jesus.

The way we relate to the Lord determines how He will relate to us. "Come near to God and he will come near to you" (James 4:8). Apart from Jesus, we can do nothing (John 15:5). It's a tragedy for us to have an active life and then at the end discover that nothing we did would last.

No leader, no author, no organization, and no set of religious disciplines can do for us what Jesus alone can do, *if we let Him.* Even the book you are now reading can merely point the way to Jesus. Divine truth becomes dynamic life only when we yield to Jesus by faith and follow Him. If the founders of the world's philosophies and religious systems were alive on earth today, they could only say, "I was." They are dead, and they can't personally help you. Jesus doesn't say, "I was." He is alive and says, "I AM." He can meet our needs today. He is alive this very moment and offers us a satisfying spiritual life *in the present tense.* "Jesus Christ is the same yesterday and today and forever" (Heb. 13:8). Past history, present reality, and future certainty all unite today in Jesus Christ, the great I AM.

The I AM statements recorded in Scripture reveal the depths of the Christian life and how God's children can go deeper by living with Jesus in the present tense. With Paul we should be able to say, "The life I now live in the body, I live by faith in the Son of God, who loved me and gave himself for me" (Gal. 2:20).

Note that phrase: "The life I *now* live."

In our memories and imaginations, we try to live in the past or in the future, but this doesn't produce a balanced or creative Christian life. Someone has said that the "good old days" are a mixture of a bad memory and a good imagination, and I agree. My past may discourage me and my future may frighten me, but "the life I now live" *today* can be enriching and encouraging because "Christ lives in me" (Gal. 2:20). As we live by faith, a day at a time, Jesus enables us to be faithful and fruitful and content.

God doesn't want us to ignore the past; the past should be a rudder to guide us, not an anchor to hold us back. Nor does He want us to neglect planning for the future, so long as we say, "If it is the Lord's will" (James 4:13–17). The better we understand our Lord's I AM statements *and by faith apply them,* the more our strength will equal our days (Deut. 33:25) and we will "run and not grow weary [and] … walk and not be faint" (Isa. 40:31). We will abide in Christ and bear fruit for His glory today—now.

That is what this book is about.

Warren W. Wiersbe

I

MOSES ASKS A QUESTION

Moses said to God, "Suppose I go to the Israelites
and say to them, 'The God of your fathers has sent
me to you,' and they ask me, 'What is his name?'
Then what shall I tell them?"

—**Exodus 3:13**

When Helen Keller was nineteen months old, she contracted an ill-
ness that left her blind and deaf for life. It was not until she was ten
years old that she began to have meaningful communication with
those around her. It occurred when her gifted teacher Anne Sullivan
taught her to say "water" as Anne spelled "water" on the palm of
her hand. From that pivotal experience, Helen Keller entered the
wonderful world of words and names, and it transformed her life.

Once Helen was accustomed to this new system of communication with others, her parents arranged for her to receive religious
instruction from the eminent Boston clergyman Phillips Brooks.
One day during her lesson, Helen said these remarkable words to

Brooks: "I knew about God before you told me, *only I didn't know His name.*"[1]

The Greek philosophers wrestled with the problem of knowing and naming God. "But the father and maker of all this universe is past finding out," Plato wrote in his *Timaeus* dialogue, "and if we found him, to tell of him to all men would be impossible." He said that God was "a geometrician," and Aristotle called God "The Prime Mover." No wonder the apostle Paul found an altar in Athens dedicated to the "Unknown God" (Acts 17:22–23). The Greek philosophers of his day were "without hope and without God in the world" (Eph. 2:12).

But thinkers in recent centuries haven't fared much better. The German philosopher Georg Wilhelm Hegel called God "the Absolute," and Herbert Spencer named Him "the Unknowable." Sigmund Freud, the founder of psychiatry, wrote in chapter 4 of his book *Totem and Taboo* (1913), "The personalized God is psychologically nothing other than a magnified father." God is a father figure but not a personal heavenly Father. British biologist Julian Huxley wrote in chapter 3 of his book *Religion without Revelation* (1957), "Operationally, God is beginning to resemble not a ruler but the last fading smile of a cosmic Cheshire cat." The fantasies described in *Alice in Wonderland* were more real to Huxley than was God Almighty!

But God wants us to know Him, because knowing God is the most important thing in life!

Salvation

To begin with, knowing God personally is the only way we sinners can be saved. Jesus said, "Now this is eternal life: that they know you, the only true God, and Jesus Christ, whom you have sent" (John 17:3). After healing a blind beggar, Jesus later searched for him and found him in the temple, and the following conversation took place:

"Do you believe in the Son of Man?" asked Jesus.

The man said, "Who is he, sir? Tell me so that I may believe in him."

Jesus replied, "You have now seen him; in fact, he is the one speaking with you."

The man said, "Lord, I believe," and he fell on his knees before Jesus (John 9:35–38). Not only was the beggar given physical sight, but his spiritual eyes were also opened (Eph. 1:18) and he received eternal life. His first response was to worship Jesus publicly where everybody could see him.

This introduces a second reason why we must know who God is and what His name is: We were created to worship and glorify Him. After all, only little joy or encouragement can come from worshipping an "unknown God." We were created in God's image that we might have fellowship with Him now and "enjoy Him forever," as the catechism says. Millions of people attend religious services faithfully each week and participate in the prescribed liturgy, but not all of them enjoy personal fellowship with God. Unlike that beggar, they have never submitted to Jesus and said, "Lord, I believe." To them, God is a distant stranger, not a loving Father. Their religious lives are a routine, not a living reality.

But there is a third reason for knowing God. Because we possess eternal life and practice biblical worship, we can experience the blessing of a transformed life. After describing the folly of idol worship, the psalmist added, "Those who make them [idols] will be like them, and so will all who trust in them" (see Ps. 115:1–8). *We become like the gods that we worship!* Worshipping a god we don't know is the equivalent of worshipping an idol, and we can have idols in our minds and imaginations as well as on our shelves.

Our heavenly Father's loving purpose for His children is that they might be "conformed to the image of his Son" (Rom. 8:29). "And just as we have borne the image of the earthly man [Adam], so shall we bear the image of the heavenly man [Jesus]" (1 Cor. 15:49). However, we should not wait until we see Jesus for this transformation to begin, because God's Holy Spirit can start changing us today. As we pray, meditate on the Word of God, experience suffering and joy, and as we witness, worship, fellowship with God's people, and serve the Lord with our spiritual gifts, the Spirit quietly works within us and transforms us to become more like our Lord Jesus Christ.

The conclusion is obvious: The better we know the Lord, the more we will love Him, and the more we love Him, the more we will worship and obey Him. As a result, we will become more like Him and experience what the apostle Peter called growing "in the grace and knowledge of our Lord and Savior Jesus Christ" (2 Peter 3:18). Paul took an incident out of the life of Moses (Ex. 34:29–35) and described it this way: "And we all, who with unveiled faces contemplate the Lord's glory, are being transformed into his image with ever-increasing glory, which comes from the Lord, who is the Spirit" (2 Cor. 3:18). Moses didn't realize that his face was radiant, but others saw it! He was being transformed.

God commands us to know Him and worship Him because He wants to give us the joyful privilege of serving and glorifying Him.

Commanding us to worship isn't God's way of going on a heavenly ego trip, because we can supply God with nothing. "If I were hungry," says the Lord, "I would not tell you, for the world is mine, and all that is in it" (Ps. 50:12). He commands worship because *we need to worship Him!* To humble ourselves before Him, to show reverence and gratitude, and to praise Him in the Spirit are essential to balanced growth in a normal Christian life. Heaven is a place of worship (Rev. 4—5), and we ought to begin to worship Him correctly right now. But unless we are growing in our knowledge of God and in our experience of His incredible grace, our worship and service will amount to very little.

Salvation, worship, personal transformation, and loving service are all part of living in the present tense and depending on our Lord and Savior. "And our fellowship is with the Father and with his Son, Jesus Christ" (1 John 1:3).

Preparation

Moses spent forty years in Egypt being "educated in all the wisdom of the Egyptians" (Acts 7:22). Then he fled for his life to Midian, where he spent the next forty years serving as a shepherd. Imagine a brilliant PhD earning a living by taking care of dumb animals! But the Lord had to humble Moses before He could exalt him and make him the deliverer of Israel. Like the church today, the nation of Israel was only a flock of sheep (Ps. 77:20; 78:52; Acts 20:28), and what the nation needed was a loving shepherd who followed the Lord and cared for His people. The Lord spent eighty years preparing Moses for forty years of faithful service. God isn't in a hurry.

The call of Moses started with the curiosity of Moses. He saw a bush that was burning but not burning up, and he paused to investigate. "Curiosity is one of the permanent and certain characteristics of a vigorous intellect," said British essayist Samuel Johnson, and Moses certainly qualified. He saw something he couldn't explain and discovered that the God of Abraham, Isaac, and Jacob was dwelling in that burning bush (Deut. 33:16). The Lord God had come to visit him.

What did that remarkable burning bush signify to Moses, and what does it signify to us? For one thing, it revealed the holiness of God; because throughout Scripture, fire is associated with the dynamic holy character of the Lord. Isaiah called God "the consuming fire" and the "everlasting burning" (Isa. 33:14; see also Heb. 12:29). Note that Moses saw this burning bush on Mount Horeb, which is Mount Sinai (Ex. 3:1; Acts 7:30–34); and when God gave Moses the law on Sinai, the mountain burned with fire (Ex. 24:15–18).

How should we respond to the holy character of God? By humbling ourselves and obeying what He commands. (See Isa. 6.) Theodore Epp wrote, "Moses was soon to discover that the essential qualifications for serving God are unshod feet and a hidden face."[2] How different a description from that of "celebrities" today, who wear expensive clothes and make sure their names and faces are kept before their adoring public. God wasn't impressed with Moses' Egyptian learning, for "the wisdom of this world is foolishness in God's sight" (1 Cor. 3:19). God's command to us is, "Humble yourselves, therefore, under God's mighty hand, that he may lift you up in due time" (1 Peter 5:6). When the Prodigal Son repented and came to his father, the father put shoes on his feet (Luke 15:22); but spiritually speaking, when believers humbly surrender to the Lord, they must remove their sandals and become bond servants of Jesus Christ.

The burning bush also reveals the grace of God, for the Lord had come down to announce the good news of Israel's salvation. He knew Moses' name and spoke to him personally (Ex. 3:4; John 10:3). He assured Moses that He saw the misery of the Jewish people in Egypt and heard their cries of pain and their prayers for help. "I am concerned about their suffering," He said. "So I have come down to rescue them" (Ex. 3:7–8). The Lord remembered and honored His covenant promises with Abraham, Isaac, and Jacob, and the time had come to deliver His people.

It was by grace that God chose Moses to be His servant. The Lord wasn't disturbed by Moses' past failures in Egypt, including the fact that even his own people had rejected his leadership (Ex. 2:11–15). Moses was now an old man who had been away from Egypt for forty years, but this didn't hinder God from using him effectively. The Lord knows how to use the weak, foolish, and despised things of the world to humiliate the wise and the strong and ultimately to defeat the mighty (1 Cor. 1:26–31). God would receive great glory as Moses magnified His name in Egypt.

Identification

If Moses was going to accomplish anything in Egypt, he needed to know the name of the Lord, because the Israelites would surely ask, "Who gave you the authority to tell us and Pharaoh what to do?"

God's reply to Moses' question was, "I AM WHO I AM." Moses told the Israelites, "I AM has sent me to you" (Ex. 3:14).

The name I AM comes from the Hebrew word *YHWH*. To pronounce this holy name, the Jews used the vowels from the name Adonai (Lord) and turned YHWH into Yahweh (LORD in our English translations). The name conveys the concept of absolute being, the One who is and whose dynamic presence works on our behalf. It conveys the meanings of "I am who and what I am, and I do not change. I am here with you and for you."

The name Yahweh (Jehovah, LORD) was known in the time of Seth (Gen. 4:26), Abraham (14:22; 15:1), Isaac (25:21–22), and Jacob (28:13; 49:18). However, the fullness of its meaning had not yet been revealed. The law of Moses warned the Jews, "You shall not misuse the name of the LORD your God, for the LORD will not hold anyone guiltless who misuses his name" (Ex. 20:7; see also Deut. 28:58). Their fear of divine judgment caused the Jewish people to avoid using the holy name Yahweh and to substitute Adonai (Lord) instead.

In nine places in the Old Testament, the Lord "filled out" or "completed" the name I AM to reveal more fully His divine nature and His gracious ministry to His people:

- Yahweh-Jireh: The LORD will provide or see to it (Gen. 22:14)

- Yahweh-Rophe: The LORD who heals (Ex. 15:26)

- Yahweh-Nissi: The LORD our banner (Ex. 17:15)

- Yahweh-M'Kaddesh: The LORD who sanctifies (Lev. 20:8)

- Yahweh-Shalom: The LORD our peace (Judg. 6:24)

- Yahweh-Rohi: The LORD my shepherd (Ps. 23:1)

- Yahweh-Sabaoth: The LORD of hosts (Ps. 46:7)

- Yahweh-Tsidkenu: The LORD our righteousness (Jer. 23:6)

- Yahweh-Shammah: The LORD is there (Ezek. 48:35)

Of course, all of these names refer to our Savior and Lord, Jesus Christ. Because He is Yahweh-Jireh, He can supply all our needs and we need not worry (Matt. 6:25–34; Phil. 4:19). As Yahweh-Rophe, He is able to heal us; and as Yahweh-Nissi, He will help us fight our battles and defeat our enemies. We belong to Yahweh-M'Kaddesh because He has set us apart for Himself (1 Cor. 6:11); and Yahweh-Shalom gives us peace in the midst of the storms of life (Isa. 26:3; Phil. 4:9). All the promises of God find their fulfillment in Jesus Christ (2 Cor. 1:20).

Yahweh-Rohi takes us to Psalm 23 and John 10, encouraging us to follow the Shepherd. The armies of heaven and earth are under the command of Yahweh-Sabaoth, and we need not panic (Josh. 5:13–15; Rev. 19:11–21). Because we have trusted

Yahweh-Tsidkenu, we have His very righteousness put to our account (2 Cor. 5:21), and our sins and iniquities are remembered no more (Heb. 10:17). Jesus is Yahweh-Shammah, "God with us" (Matt. 1:23), and He will be with us always, even to the very end of the age (Matt. 28:20). "Never will I leave you; never will I forsake you" is still His guarantee (Heb. 13:5).

In His incarnation, Jesus came down to earth, not as a burning bush but as "a tender shoot, and like a root out of dry ground" (Isa. 53:1–2; see also Phil. 2:5–11). He became a human, a man, for us (John 1:14); He became obedient unto death for us and became sin for us (2 Cor. 5:21). Jesus became a curse for us and on the cross bore the curse of the law for us who have broken God's law (Gal. 3:13–14). And one day "we shall be like him, for we shall see him as he is" (1 John 3:2)!

What is God's name?

His name is I AM—and that is also the name of His Son, Jesus Christ, our Lord!

2

THE APOSTLE JOHN PROVIDES
SOME ANSWERS

We would have expected the apostle Matthew to deal with the I AM statements in his gospel, because he wrote especially for the Jews; but the Holy Spirit selected John, the disciple whom Jesus loved, to share these truths with us. But why John? Because John wrote his gospel to prove that Jesus Christ is the I AM, the very Son of God. "Jesus performed many other signs in the presence of his disciples, which are not recorded in this book. But these are written that you may believe that Jesus is the Messiah, the Son of God, and that by believing you may have life in his name" (John 20:30–31). John wrote as a theologian to prove the deity of Jesus Christ, but he also wrote as an evangelist, urging his readers to put their faith in Jesus and receive eternal life. Besides his own testimony in John 20:30–31, John quotes seven other witnesses who affirm that Jesus Christ is God the Son:

- **John the Baptist:** "I myself have seen, and have testified that this is the Son of God" (John 1:34 NASB).

- **Nathanael:** "Rabbi, you are the Son of God" (John 1:49).

- **The Samaritans:** "Now we have heard for ourselves, and we know that this man really is the Savior of the world" (John 4:42).

- **Peter:** "We have come to believe and to know that you are the Holy One of God" (John 6:69).

- **The healed blind beggar:** "Then the man said, 'Lord, I believe,' and he worshiped him" (John 9:38).

- **Martha, sister of Mary and Lazarus:** "Yes, Lord ... I believe that you are the Messiah, the Son of God, who was to come into the world" (John 11:27).

- **Thomas the apostle:** "Thomas said to him, 'My Lord and my God!'" (John 20:28).

Along with His I AM statements, Jesus Himself declared that He was the Son of God sent from heaven by the Father. Read carefully our Lord's statements in John 5:24–27 and 10:22–39, and His prayer recorded in John 17. Some students of John's gospel believe that our Lord's words in John 4:26 and 8:24, 28, 58, as well as 13:19 and 18:5–6, are all "theologically loaded" and affirm His deity as the great I AM. Did He say to the Samaritan woman, "I AM is speaking to you"? Did He warn the unbelieving Jews that "if you do not believe that I AM he, you will indeed die in your sins" (see 8:24)? One of the key words in John's gospel is *life*, used at least thirty-six times; and the seven I AM statements all relate to John's theme of spiritual life in Christ. Jesus called Himself "the bread of life" (6:35, 48, see also verses 51, 58) and "the light of life" (8:12). Through the Word we can "feed" on Him and follow Him and experience this promised life. He is the door (gate) of the sheep that enables us to "go in and out" and enjoy freedom and abundant life (see 10:7–10). He is the Good Shepherd who lays down His life so that we might have eternal life (10:11, 15, 17–18). "I am the resurrection and the life," Jesus told Martha (11:25–26; see also 5:24), and to the disciples He said, "I am the way and the truth and the life" (14:6). Jesus is "the true vine," and we are the branches. Because of the life He imparts to us as we abide in Him, we are able to bear fruit that glorifies Him (15:1–5).

In His I AM statements, Jesus not only tells us who He is, but He also tells us what He can do for us and what we can become through Him. If we are spiritually hungry, He offers us the bread of life. To those walking in darkness, He gives the light of life; and we need not fear death, because He is the resurrection and the life. Can we be sure of going to heaven? Yes, because He is "the way and the truth and the life" (14:6). Can our lives be fruitful for His glory? Yes, if we abide in Him and draw upon His life.

In Jesus Christ, the great I AM, we have all that we need!

3

THE BREAD OF LIFE

Do not work for food that spoils, but for food that endures to eternal life.

—**John 6:27**

Why spend money on what is not bread, and your labor on what does not satisfy?

—**Isaiah 55:2**

For the bread of God is the bread that comes down from heaven and gives life to the world.

—**John 6:33**

I am the bread of life. Whoever comes to me will never go hungry, and whoever believes in me will never be thirsty.

—**John 6:35**

Very truly I tell you, whoever believes has eternal
life. I am the bread of life.

—John 6:47–48

I am the living bread that came down from heaven.
Whoever eats of this bread will live forever.

—John 6:51

The Spirit gives life; the flesh counts for nothing.
The words I have spoken to you—they are full of
the Spirit and life.

—John 6:63

The Word became flesh and made his dwelling
among us. We have seen his glory, the glory of the
one and only Son, who came from the Father, full
of grace and truth.

—John 1:14

Only two of our Lord's miracles are recorded in all four gospels: His
own resurrection and His feeding of the five thousand (Matthew 14,
Mark 6, Luke 9, and John 6). In their accounts of the feeding of the
five thousand, all four writers tell us *what* Jesus did, but only Mark
tells us *why* He did it—because of His compassion for the crowd
(Mark 6:34).

In John's record, Jesus reveals His compassion in three ways: He feeds the hungry crowd (John 6:1–15), He delivers His disciples from danger (6:16–24), and He offers the bread of life to a world of hungry sinners (6:25–71). Jesus did this miracle not only to meet human needs, but also that He might deliver a profound sermon about "the bread of life," a sermon our lost world needs to hear today. What the world needs is Jesus, for He alone is the bread of life.

Compassion for the Crowd

People commit a serious blunder when they decide that the Bible is an outdated book about an ancient people who lived in a backward culture, and therefore the Bible has nothing to say to us today. But the reason most people ignore or totally dismiss the Bible isn't because the cast of characters and the script seem radically different from life today, but because *Bible people and modern people are so very much alike!* On September 2, 1851, Henry David Thoreau wrote in his journal, "The more we know about the ancients, the more we find that they were like the moderns." When we read the Bible with a sincere desire to learn, we soon meet ourselves in its pages and see ourselves as we really are, and the experience isn't always enjoyable.

One Sunday, I was a guest preacher at a church, and after the morning service a gentleman approached me and said, "Who told you about me?"

"I'm sorry, sir," I replied, "but I don't even know you. Nobody told me anything about you or anybody else in this church. I'm a stranger here."

"Well, somebody must have told you something," he said and

turned and walked off very angrily. He had met himself in the Bible, seen his dirty face in the mirror, and had gone away to try to forget what he looked like (James 1:22–24).

The more you consider the crowd that followed Jesus, the more you discover how much they resemble people today. Crowds are crowds and people are people whether they are fans at a soccer game, teens at a rock concert, or customers at a shopping mall. The people in the crowd Jesus fed on the eastern shore of the Sea of Galilee were just like you and me and the people in our "crowd" today.

They were hungry. Hunger is something God has built into the human body to remind us to eat, because without food and water, we will die. But there is a deeper spiritual hunger in the human heart that can never be satisfied with anything other than God Himself and the gifts of grace He shares with us. "Thou hast made us for Thyself," wrote Augustine, "and our hearts are restless until they rest in Thee."

How tragic that most people ignore God, the only One who can satisfy their deepest hungers, and spend money on substitutes that don't last and can never give them joy. "Why spend money on what is not bread and your labor on what does not satisfy?" asked the prophet Isaiah. You can buy sleep but not peace, entertainment but not joy, reputation but not character. "All the unhappiness of men arises from one single fact," wrote the French philosopher Pascal, "that they cannot stay quietly in their own chamber" (*Pensees*, sect. 2, #139). We can't get along with others because we can't get along with ourselves, and we can never get along with ourselves until we are in fellowship with the heavenly Father through faith in Jesus Christ. In this world of noise and crowds, silence and solitude are enemies to human enjoyment and must be avoided. Restless people must get lost in the crowd and keep busy in a multitude of activities in order to escape the demands of life.

They were seekers. During the first year of His ministry, before the official opposition began, Jesus was immensely popular and great crowds followed Him. However, the crowds did not impress Jesus, nor did He cater to them, because He knows what is in the human heart (John 2:25). Anybody can join a crowd and go with the flow, but it takes courage to stand alone for the truth and obey it.

It looked as though that crowd was seeking spiritual enrichment from Jesus, but the Lord knew better. Most of them wanted to see something sensational, like a miracle, while others were concerned about something to eat (John 6:26). A generation later, the Roman satirist Juvenal wrote that the Romans "longed eagerly for just two things—bread and circuses," but this Jewish crowd was just as bad, and so are many crowds today. The apostle John would have called them "worldly" because they focused on "the lust of the flesh and the lust of the eyes and the boastful pride of life" (1 John 2:16 NASB).

Like the crowds today, *they asked questions but rejected the Lord's answers.* If you are honestly seeking the truth, asking questions of wise people is a good thing to do; but be sure to ask the right questions and be willing to act upon the answers. Truth is a tool to build with, not a toy to play with. Jesus said, "Anyone who chooses to do the will of God will find out whether my teaching comes from God" (John 7:17).

Their first question was, "Rabbi, when did you get here?" (6:25). After feeding the crowd, Jesus had sent the disciples to Capernaum in the ship while He remained behind to pray. He saw the disciples struggling in the storm, so He walked out on the sea to rescue them. Together they landed at Capernaum, where some of the crowd had already arrived. The crowd knew that Jesus had not gotten into the ship with the disciples when the boat cast off, nor had He walked around the lake to Capernaum with any of the crowd, so no wonder they were perplexed!

Their additional questions further revealed their spiritual ignorance and selfish appetites. "What must we do to do the works God requires?" (6:28). Jesus told them to believe in Him, but instead of believing, they asked for a sign (vv. 30–31). Yes, He had just fed thousands of people, but they wanted a sign *from heaven*. After all, didn't Moses bring bread from heaven? Jesus told them that He was the true bread that had come down from heaven, and they immediately disputed His claims (vv. 32–59). People still ask questions and hope the answers will be what they think they already know. They need to pray this prayer by an anonymous believer:

> From the cowardice that shrinks from new truths,
> From the laziness that is content with half-truths,
> From the arrogance that thinks it knows all truth,
> O God of truth, deliver us!

They were spiritually blind. They could not grasp what Jesus was talking about. He was simply saying, just as they ate food and it became part of them to sustain physical life, so they must by faith receive Him into their hearts and experience spiritual life, the eternal life that comes only from God. Then they will be satisfied.

THE BREAD OF LIFE

It's obvious that Jesus was speaking metaphorically in picture language because He knew it was against the Mosaic law for Jews to eat human flesh or to drink blood (Gen. 9:4; Lev. 3:17; 7:26–27; 17:10–16). But the crowd took His words literally and missed the whole point of His message. As we continue our study, we will discover that this blindness to spiritual truth is one of the important themes of John's gospel. Like many people today, the crowd thought that salvation was the result of their own good works (John 6:28). They could not understand that it was a gift from God in response to faith (Eph. 2:8–9).

They wanted immediate relief from their troubles at no cost to themselves. Life was difficult, and they were excited to find somebody who could so easily meet their needs. They thought perhaps Jesus was the prophet that Moses promised in Deuteronomy 18:17–18, but then they decided they should make Him king (John 6:14–15). If Jesus were king, He could defeat the Romans and establish the kingdom of Israel again. Like many people today, they had a "commercial attitude" toward Jesus and wanted Him to meet their personal needs, *but they didn't want Him to deal with their sins and change their hearts!* Jesus says "I AM" and not "I will be whatever you want Me to be." One person wants Jesus only as a religious teacher but not as Lord and Savior, while others want Him to give them business success so they can become wealthy. But we must accept Him just as He is, and not receive Him in bits and pieces. If we don't accept Him as He is, we don't receive Him at all.

They wanted to "do" something to be saved rather than to believe in the Savior (John 6:27–29). This was an evidence of pride and spiritual ignorance, for every adult Jew should have known from the Scriptures, read faithfully in the synagogues, that nobody is saved by good works. The Mosaic sacrificial system at the temple spoke vividly of the innocent dying for the guilty, and Old Testament chapters like Psalms 32 and 51, as well as Isaiah 53, clearly taught the wonder of God's grace and the need for sinners to trust Him for salvation. The very fact that God bypassed the other nations and chose the Jews is evidence that salvation is by grace and not by merit.

They didn't deserve anything, yet in His compassion Jesus fed the crowd, knowing full well they would soon desert Him. "He causes his sun to rise on the evil and the good, and sends rain on the righteous and the unrighteous" (Matt. 5:45). Life itself is a gift from God, and so are the means to sustain that life, but most people take all of this for granted. Paul reminded the Greek philosophers in Athens that God "gives everyone life and breath and everything else" (Acts 17:25). The Father sent His Son "to be the Savior of the world" (1 John 4:14), and Jesus alone gives us the bread of life; but if we don't receive Him within, just as we receive our food, He cannot save us.

Crowds are good at asking questions, but they don't always take seriously the answers the Lord gives them, nor do they ponder the truths He teaches them. Jesus had already warned the Twelve that, in spite of seeing His miracles and hearing His teaching, the crowds could not be trusted. "Though seeing, they do not see; though hearing, they do not hear or understand" (Matt. 13:13). The crowds wanted an earthly kingdom, but Jesus offered them a heavenly new birth.

Some years ago, as I was meditating on John 6, a little poem resulted:

No problem is too large, when Jesus is in charge.

No gift is too small, if you give Him your all.

Compassion for His Struggling Apostles

As the disciples gathered up the pieces of bread and fish that were left over from the miraculous meal (Mark 6:30–44), they must have overheard what some of the men in the crowd were saying to one another:

"Jesus may be the prophet that Moses promised would come. Let's make Him king. See how easily we were all fed and satisfied and it didn't cost us anything. Perhaps He could even get rid of the Romans and give us our freedom."

Of course, this undisciplined crowd was completely unprepared to confront the Romans and take over the government, and further-more, that wasn't the plan Jesus had in mind. The Twelve frequently discussed matters concerning the kingdom and had debated among themselves which one of them was the greatest, so a popular uprising might have fit right in with their ideas. (See Acts 1:6–9.) This is why Jesus compelled the apostles to get into the ship and sail back to Capernaum while He dismissed the crowd and went into the hills to pray. Danger was in the air, and He had to protect them. Jesus knew that the storm was coming and deliberately sent the apostles into that storm rather than allow them to be influenced by the unbeliev-ing, politically minded people in the crowd. *The Twelve were safer in a ship on the stormy sea than on land with a group of spiritually blind, selfishly motivated people!*

As Jesus prayed, He kept His eyes on the ship and saw that the

Twelve were in danger; so He went directly to them, walking on the water. (This is when Peter walked with Him on the water in Matthew 14:25–33.) When Jesus and Peter got into the ship, the storm ceased and immediately the boat was at the shore in Capernaum. What a dramatic series of miracles! He fed more than five thousand people with a small lunch. He walked on the water and enabled Peter to walk on the water. He stilled the storm and instantly brought the ship to shore.

I cannot help but see in these events a picture of the church of Jesus Christ in this tempestuous and dangerous world. As we obey the commands of the Master, we sometimes find ourselves caught in storms and seemingly make no progress. But our Master is interceding for us in heaven; He comes to us at just the right time. He enables us to overcome the storm and finally reach our intended destination.

Some of the people wanted to make Jesus king, *but He already was king!* "The LORD sits enthroned over the flood; the LORD is enthroned as King forever. The LORD gives strength to his people; the LORD blesses his people with peace" (Ps. 29:10–11). "You rule over the surging sea; when its waves mount up, you still them" (Ps. 89:9). "He stilled the storm to a whisper; the waves of the sea were hushed" (Ps. 107:29).

In the years following, when the apostles experienced storms of persecution, no doubt they remembered this unique experience and it encouraged them. After all, they were not in the storm because they disobeyed God, as was Jonah (Jonah 1—2), but because they had *obeyed.* They could say, "The Lord brought us here and He will see us through." Jesus said to them, "It is I," which literally is "I am"

(John 6:20). If we are in the will of God, Jesus is with us and we need not be afraid.

Compassion for a Lost World

Jesus is "full of grace and truth," and "grace and truth came through Jesus Christ" (John 1:14, 17). In His grace, Jesus fed the hungry multitude on the hillside, and then in the Capernaum synagogue He shared the truth that the miracle conveyed. He offered them the bread of life, but many of the people refused the gift, walked away, and followed Him no more (6:66). This is the first of three crises recorded in John's gospel, a subject we will discuss more fully in chapter 8.

The metaphor. In this message, Jesus called Himself "the bread from heaven" (John 6:32, 41, 50, 58), "the bread of God" (v. 33), "the bread of life" (vv. 35, 48), and "the living bread" (v. 51). He was using bread, a familiar material object, to teach a spiritual truth: You receive bread into your body and it sustains life, but receiving Jesus into your heart by faith gives you eternal life. Later He included "drinking blood" (vv. 53–56), which obviously was not to be taken literally any more than "eating his flesh" was to be taken literally.

To "eat" something means to assimilate it and make it a part of your physical being. But language uses the metaphor of *eating* to describe the process of understanding and receiving statements expressed in words. We say things like, "Well, I'll have to digest what you just said" or "I can't swallow that" or "That's food for thought." A pastor might say, "My congregation is so young in the faith, I have to spoon-feed them." A businessman says to his staff, "Now, here's a program you can sink your teeth into." A student says, "I really devoured that book." Nobody takes this literally.

Scripture uses similar metaphorical language in describing our relationship to God and His truth. "Taste and see that the LORD is good" (Ps. 34:8). "How sweet are your words to my taste, sweeter than honey to my mouth" (Ps. 119:103). "When your words came, I ate them; they were my joy and my heart's delight" (Jer. 15:16). "Like newborn babies, crave pure spiritual milk, so that by it you may grow up in your salvation, now that you have tasted that the Lord is good " (1 Peter 2:2–3; see also Heb. 5:11–14). "People do not live on bread alone, but on every word that comes from the mouth of God" (Matt. 4:4). The prophet Ezekiel and the apostle John were each commanded to eat a scroll of the Word of God so they could proclaim God's truth (Ezek. 2:1—3:3; Rev. 10).

The misunderstanding. Instead of discerning the deeper spiritual meaning of the metaphor, the crowd took it literally and reacted negatively. "How can we eat his flesh and drink his blood?" they asked. You find this spiritual blindness throughout the gospel of John. When Jesus spoke about His death and resurrection, they thought He was referring to destroying and rebuilding the Jewish temple (John 2:13–22). When Jesus taught about sinners being "born again," Nicodemus thought only of physical birth (3:1–4). And when He talked to the Samaritan woman about satisfying spiritual thirst, she thought He meant satisfying physical thirst by drinking water from the well (4:10–15).

Even our Lord's own disciples didn't always understand the spiritual truths Jesus tried to impart (John 4:31–38; 11:11–16; 13:6–11). In fact, there are sincere religious people today who interpret the "eating and drinking" metaphor literally and think that Jesus was referring to the Lord's Supper (Eucharist, Communion), but this interpretation is certainly not what Jesus had in mind.

To begin with, why would Jesus discuss the Lord's Supper, a "family" meal for believers, with a crowd of rebellious unbelieving Jews? He hadn't even mentioned it to His own disciples! Until Jesus instituted the supper with His disciples in the upper room, *nobody in the Old Testament or the four gospels had ever participated in it!* Does this mean that nobody during that long period of time was saved? We know that Abraham, Isaac, Jacob, Rahab, David, the prophets, Elizabeth and Zechariah, Mary and Joseph, and the woman at the well were saved, yet they had never participated in the Lord's Supper. The thief on the cross never partook of the bread and cup, yet Jesus assured him that he was going to heaven (Luke 23:39–43). Does Jesus reject the soldier who trusts Christ during his last minutes on the battlefield, or the patient dying in the hospital bed, because they can't share in the Lord's Supper? I think not. Jesus said, "Very truly I tell you, whoever believes has eternal life" (John 6:47). It is faith in Jesus Christ and faith alone that saves sinners (Eph. 2:8–9).

Paul's instructions concerning the Lord's Supper (1 Cor. 11:23–32) make it clear that the meal is only for believers. We don't partake in order to have our sins forgiven. Believers are to confess their sins *before they partake* lest they invite discipline from the Lord. Unbelievers don't come to the table to be saved; they shouldn't come at all! And true believers confess their sins first and then come to the table, because the eating and drinking will not cleanse them. The way to cleansing is obedience to the direction in 1 John 1:9.

How, then, do we "eat" His flesh and "drink" His blood? *By believing in Jesus Christ and receiving His Word into our hearts.* Jesus said, "It is the Spirit who gives life; the flesh profits nothing; the words that I have spoken to you are spirit and are life" (John 6:63 NASB). "The Word became flesh" at the incarnation (John 1:14), and believers "feed on" Jesus, the living Word, as they meditate on the written Word. Peter got the message, for when Jesus asked the Twelve if they would also go away with the crowd, He received the answer He expected. "Lord, to whom shall we go? You have the words of eternal life. We have come to believe and to know that you are the Holy One of God" (John 6:68–69). Believe in Jesus and receive the Word!

When I trusted Christ as my Lord and Savior, the Spirit gave me an insatiable appetite for the Word of God, and the Bible has been my "spiritual diet" since 1945. I "feed on" the Lord Jesus Christ daily through His Word, and I can say with Job, "I have treasured the words of his mouth more than my daily bread" (Job 23:12). That Jesus would compare Himself to such a common article as a loaf of bread shows the depth of His humiliation. It also shows us that *we cannot have life without Him.* Bread is called "the staff of life" because for centuries it has been the primary food of most people. Jesus Christ is "the bread of life," and we cannot have spiritual life— eternal life—without Him.

The miracles. Instead of accepting their Messiah, the crowd began to debate with Jesus. They contrasted Christ's miracle of feeding the five thousand with the miracle of the manna in Moses' day, when God provided "bread from heaven" (Ex. 16; see also Ps. 78:24). Jesus provided bread for the Jews only once, but Moses fed them six days a week for thirty-eight years. Furthermore, Moses fed an entire nation, but Jesus fed only several thousand people. Jesus borrowed a child's lunch to provide the bread, but Moses brought down the bread from heaven.

But Jesus pointed out that their perspective was totally backward! His miracle was far greater than anything Moses did, for the manna was but a picture of the Son of God who would come down from heaven to be the bread of life. In His synagogue sermon, Jesus contrasted Moses and the Old Testament manna with Himself as the bread of life. The phrase "bread of life" can mean "living bread" or "bread that gives life." This summary shows how great Jesus is and how imperative it is for sinners to trust Him and receive eternal life.

The Old Testament manna	Jesus, the bread of life
Met a physical need temporarily	Meets a spiritual need eternally
Only *sustained* physical life	*Imparts* eternal life
For only one nation, Israel	For the whole world (John 6:51)
For only thirty-eight years	From Adam to the end of time
At no cost to the Lord	At great cost: Jesus had to die
Only delayed physical death	Conquered spiritual death
God sent a gift	God sent the Giver of all gifts

Five times in His sermon Jesus affirmed that He had "come down from heaven" (John 6:33, 38, 50, 51, 58), and twice the crowd

quoted Him (vv. 41, 42); and five times He said that the Father had
sent Him (vv. 29, 38, 39, 44, 57). These ten affirmations from Jesus
point to one tremendous truth: He is the Son of God who came
down from heaven and was sent by the Father. The Old Testament
manna came down from heaven because the Father sent it, and it
became a type of the Lord Jesus Christ.

To begin with, the manna was a mysterious substance that
could not be explained. In fact, the very word *manna* is a form of
the Hebrew question *man hu,* which means "What is it?" (see Ex.
16:15). Paul called Jesus "the mystery of godliness" (1 Tim. 3:16
NKJV). Since Jesus had existed in eternity long before Mary was even
born, He could not be born of natural generation. He was conceived
by the Holy Spirit in Mary's virgin womb (Luke 1:26–38) and therefore was both human and divine, the eternal sinless Son of God. We
can't explain the mystery of godliness, but we thank God for it and
share in the blessing!

Exodus 16:14 describes the manna as "thin flakes like frost on
the ground," and verse 31 informs us it was like a small white seed
and tasted like honey. "White" speaks of purity and "small" speaks
of humility, both of which describe Jesus. God sent the manna just
where His people were camping, and it wasn't necessary to search
for it. In His incarnation, Jesus came where we are and became what
we are, except that He was sinless. The manna came down at night,
even as Jesus came into a world dark with sin (Matt. 4:15–16). The
manna was not defiled because it came on the dew, just as Jesus was
in this world but not of this world because the Holy Spirit filled
Him, guided Him, and empowered Him (John 17:13–18; Num.
11:9).

For thirty-eight years, the manna was sufficient to satisfy the physical needs of the Israelites. All they had to do was get up early ("Seek the LORD while he may be found," Isa. 55:6), stoop ("Humble yourselves, therefore," 1 Peter 5:6), gather the heavenly bread, and eat it ("Taste and see that the LORD is good," Ps. 34:8). *If they did not gather the manna, they walked on it!* (See Heb. 10:29.) The crowd listening to Jesus walked away from the bread of life. What a tragedy! They rejected Jesus and went back to laboring and spending money for bread that could not satisfy. People are still doing that today. Even though Jesus gave His life for the salvation of the world (John 6:51), the world has rejected Him. But the Father is still using the Word of God to draw sinners to His Son (vv. 44–45). Those who come by faith (vv. 35, 37, 44–45, 65) will not be rejected (v. 37). God our Savior wants "all people to be saved" (1 Tim. 2:4) and does not want "anyone to perish, but everyone to come to repentance" (2 Peter 3:9).

The masquerade. The remarkable events recorded in John 6 do not end with Jesus commending Peter but with Jesus warning Judas (vv. 66–71). In the original Greek text, Judas Iscariot is mentioned eight times in the gospel of John (6:71; 12:4; 13:2, 26, 29; 18:2, 3, 5), and this is the first instance. Peter thought he was speaking for himself and the other apostles when he affirmed his loyalty to Jesus, but he and the other ten apostles had no idea that Judas was a deceiver and would betray Jesus to His enemies. Of course, Jesus knew and called Judas a devil (accuser, slanderer). During the time Judas was with Jesus, he had ample opportunity to study the Master carefully, listen to His messages, and see His miracles; *and yet in the end, he rejected Christ and betrayed Him!*

Judas carried on his religious masquerade so effectively that none of his fellow apostles knew he was an unbeliever and a deceiver.

When it comes to making a decision about Jesus Christ, we have three choices: (1) believe in Him and be saved, as did eleven of the apostles; (2) reject Him but pretend to be saved, as did Judas; or (3) reject Him openly and walk away, as did the multitude. In His parable about the wheat and tares (Matt. 13:24–30, 36–43), Jesus made it clear that there are counterfeit Christians like Judas mixed in with the authentic children of God, but at the end of the age they will be exposed and condemned. Satan is a counterfeiter who can pass for an angel of light and so can his servants (2 Cor. 11:13–15). Judas did not lose his salvation (if such a thing were possible) because he was never saved to begin with. No wonder Jesus warned about false believers (Matt. 7:21–23) and Paul wrote, "Examine yourselves to see whether you are in the faith; test yourselves" (2 Cor. 13:5).

We live in a world filled with hungry people who are searching for reality and cannot find it. They are spending their money on that which is not bread and their labor on that which does not satisfy (Isa. 55:2). Why? Because we who are enjoying the feast have not told them about Jesus, the bread of life, or have not helped to make it possible for others to tell them. One day they will say to us, "For I was hungry and you gave me nothing to eat," and our Lord will say, "Truly I tell you, whatever you did not do for one of the least of these, you did not do for me" (Matt. 25:42, 45).

And what will *we* say?

4

THE LIGHT OF THE WORLD

I am the light of the world. Whoever follows me will never walk in darkness, but will have the light of life.

—**John 8:12**

As long as it is day, we must do the works of him who sent me. Night is coming, when no one can work. While I am in the world, I am the light of the world.

—**John 9:4–5**

Now the earth was formless and empty, darkness was over the surface of the deep, and the Spirit of God was hovering over the waters. And God said, "Let there be light," and there was light. God saw

that the light was good, and he separated the light
from the darkness. God called the light "day," and
the darkness he called "night." And there was evening, and there was morning—the first day.

—**Genesis 1:2–5**

For God, who said, "Let light shine out of darkness," made his light shine in our hearts to give us
the light of the knowledge of God's glory displayed
in the face of Christ.

—**2 Corinthians 4:6**

In him was life, and that life was the light of all
people. The light shines in the darkness, and the
darkness has not overcome it.

—**John 1:4–5**

This is the verdict: Light has come into the world,
but people loved darkness instead of light because
their deeds were evil.

—**John 3:19**

You are going to have the light just a little while
longer. Walk while you have the light, before darkness overtakes you. Those who walk in the dark do

not know where they are going. Put your trust in
the light while you have the light, so that you may
become children of light.

—John 12:35–36

The deepest darkness I ever experienced was during a tour of
Mammoth Cave in Kentucky. The group had just entered a much
deeper cavern and our guide informed us that the lights were about
to be turned off. We were instructed not to move until the lights were
turned on again, and nobody had a problem obeying that order! For
the first time I understood what Moses meant when he described the
tenth plague in Egypt as "darkness that can be felt" (Ex. 10:21–23).
It's impossible to explain it, but we could feel the darkness and were
happy to see the lights come on again.

The people living on Planet Earth are very familiar with the
sequence of day and night, so it's no surprise that in many languages
light and *darkness* are used as metaphors. Light usually symbolizes
what is good and darkness what is bad. For example, if you don't
understand what's going on, you are "in the dark"; if you do understand, you are "enlightened." In Scripture, light speaks of God ("God
is light," 1 John 1:5), and the darkness speaks of sin and Satan (John
3:19–21; Acts 26:18). Sinners perform "deeds of darkness" (Rom.
13:12), while God's people should live as "children of light" (Eph.
5:8–13). Jesus called hell "outer darkness" (Matt. 8:12; 25:30 NASB),
but Revelation 21:25 tells us that there will be no night in heaven.
Unbelievers are lost in the darkness (John 12:46), while believers
have been called out of darkness and "into his wonderful light"
(1 Peter 2:9).

When John the Baptist appeared on the scene and announced the arrival of the Messiah, "he came as a witness to testify concerning that light [Jesus]" (John 1:7). *The only people you must tell that the light is shining are blind people!* Many people believed John, repented of their sins, and had their eyes opened to truth, but the religious leaders of the nation remained in darkness. They thought that they could see and that the common people were ignorant, but it was quite the opposite. The common people believed John and followed Jesus, while the "spiritual leaders" resisted God's truth (Matt. 21:23–27). Some of them said that Jesus was a drunk, a glutton, and a demon-possessed man.

As in that day, so today: The most dangerous darkness in our "enlightened age" is the dense spiritual darkness that blinds the minds and controls the hearts of people who have never trusted Christ or who claim to know Him but don't follow Him. Jesus came to dispel spiritual darkness, and to do so, He had to endure the darkness and the suffering of the cross. As the prophet Isaiah described it, "the people walking in darkness have seen a great light; on those living in the land of deep darkness a light has dawned" (Isa. 9:2; see also Matt. 4:15–16).

In order to live as "children of light," we must understand and personally apply the truths Jesus shared when He said, "I am the light of the world." Let's consider three aspects of this statement from our Lord.

The Setting

The context of John 7—9 is the celebration of the annual Festival of Tabernacles (John 7:2–3, 14, 37), which the Jewish people observed for eight days in the seventh month of their calendar, which would be sometime in our mid-September to mid-October (Lev. 23:33–44). It was not only a time of joyful thanksgiving for the harvest, but it was also a celebration of God's care of their ancestors during the years they wandered in the wilderness and lived in temporary dwellings. During the week of the festival, many people lived in booths made of tree branches set on the roofs of their houses. Jerusalem was filled with visitors and alive with celebration—singing and dancing, torch parades, and even people marching around the city walls in imitation of Israel's great victory at the city of Jericho (Josh. 6).

Early each morning during that week, some priests would carry water from the Pool of Siloam and pour it out on the west side of the brazen altar in the temple court. This reminded the people how God had provided water for their ancestors during their difficult journey to Canaan. This ritual should also have reminded them of the words of Isaiah: "With joy you will draw water from the wells of salvation" (Isa. 12:3). On the last day of the festival when the water was poured out, Jesus used the event as an opportunity to tell the people that they could satisfy their spiritual thirst by trusting Him and receiving the gift of the Spirit: "Let anyone who is thirsty come to me and drink" (John 7:37–39).

At night during the week, the priests lit four large candelabra in the court of the women, and the glow from the light could be seen across the city. These lamps were reminders to the Jews of the pillar of fire by which God led Israel through the darkness. But they were also a symbol of the cloud of God's glory that led the nation by day and hovered over the tabernacle when the people camped (Ex. 13:21–22; 40:34–38; Num. 14:14). "The LORD is my light and my salvation" (Ps. 27:1). "Your word is a lamp to my feet and a light for my path" (Ps. 119:105). "Arise, shine, for your light has come, and the glory of the LORD rises upon you" (Isa. 60:1). Did the celebrants in Jesus' day think of these verses?

The people who knew the Scriptures would remember that the prophet Ezekiel had described the glory of God departing from the temple in Jerusalem before the city was destroyed by the Babylonians. (See Ezek. 9—11.) As in the time of Samuel the prophet, they could say, "Ichabod—the glory has departed" (see 1 Sam. 4:21). When the priests were putting out the lamps at the end of the festival, perhaps that's when Jesus cried out, "I am the light of the world!"

The Meaning

It was proper for the Jewish people to observe this feast because God had commanded it. However, it was tragic that, in their many joyful activities, *they were ignoring the Son of God, who alone could bless them!* Jesus had to stand up and shout to get their attention. Divine truth had been replaced by man-made tradition. Nowhere did the Lord command the priests to light huge candelabra or to pour out water at the altar. There was nothing essentially wicked about either activity; but unless the priests and people lifted their minds and hearts to the Lord and experienced changed lives, those traditions were futile. When man's tradition replaces God's Word, then illusion replaces reality. We glory in the past but never grow in the present.

Great value can be found in celebrating meaningful traditions that are handed down from generation to generation. Every nation, city, and family has them. The English word *tradition* comes from the Latin *traditio* and simply means "to hand over." When Paul commended the believers in Corinth for "holding to the traditions" (1 Cor. 11:2), he was referring to the commands he had received from the Lord and had faithfully passed on to them, including how to observe the Lord's Supper (vv. 23–26). The tradition itself is not wrong, *but it is wrong to observe it in a meaningless and routine way and to ignore the Son of God.* The late theologian and church historian Jaroslav Pelikan wrote, "Tradition is the living faith of the dead; traditionalism is the dead faith of the living."[1] In our Lord's time, the Pharisees practiced and protected their legalistic traditions and criticized Jesus for neglecting them, but Jesus rejected both their traditions and the legalism behind them (Mark 7:1–23). But before we criticize the Pharisees too severely, let's examine our own churches and see if perchance our practices may represent "the dead faith of the living." Godly tradition, born out of biblical truth, loving ministry, and deep spiritual experience, is too precious to be abused or ignored.

As the priests extinguished the candelabra in the court of the women and thus ended the festival, Jesus called out, "I am the light of the world. Whoever follows me will never walk in darkness, but will have the light of life" (John 8:12). He didn't condemn their tradition; He simply asked them to allow that tradition to point to Him. They had light in their temple but spiritual darkness in their minds and hearts. In spite of their joyful religious festivities, the priests and people were dead in their sins, and the festival itself could never give them life. Jesus offered them life—eternal life—if only they would trust Him and follow Him.

In short, Jesus wanted them to have lasting blessing *in the present tense,* and only He could give them that blessing. The Jews were only looking back and remembering what God had done for their ancestors, when God was willing *that very day* to give them the water of life and the light of life! "Light" is one of the names of the Messiah, based on the phrase "light dwells with him [God]" in Daniel 2:22, and surely the Jewish religious leaders knew this. They also knew the prophecy in Malachi 4:2: "But for you who revere my name, the sun of righteousness will rise with healing in its rays." Here they were, pouring out water, lighting lamps, living in booths, and having a joyful time, *yet they really had nothing to celebrate because they had ignored Jesus.*

Jesus knew the appalling spiritual condition of the people, especially that of the religious leaders. "Though seeing, they do not see; though hearing, they do not hear or understand.... For this people's heart has become calloused; they hardly hear with their ears, and they have closed their eyes" (Matt. 13:13, 15; see also Isa. 6:9–10). They didn't know who Jesus was, *nor were they willing to investigate* (John 8:25). They claimed God as their spiritual Father (v. 41) and Abraham as their ancestral father (v. 39), when in reality Satan was their father (v. 44). Israel faced a much greater judgment than the "unclean" Gentiles, because they had been given more light and yet rejected it (vv. 39–45).

These Jewish religious leaders could see the sun in the heavens (John 8:2), but they did not know the Son who came down from heaven to save them. They didn't love Jesus (v. 42), understand Him (v. 43), believe in Him (v. 45), or honor Him (v. 49), nor did they really know the Father (vv. 54–55). Instead of listening to Jesus carefully and believing His words, they argued with Him, and as a consequence, they rejected Him. The darkness of unbelief and ungodliness was overcoming them.

In our physical world, the sun is "the light of the world," but in the spiritual kingdom, Jesus is *the* Light and there is no other. Everything in our galaxy depends on the sun, and without it, there would be only darkness and death. Satan masquerades as an angel of light (2 Cor. 11:13–15), but Jesus is the only true Light (John 1:9). "For there is one God, and one mediator also between God and men, the man Christ Jesus" (1 Tim. 2:5 NASB). If you have trusted Christ as your Savior and Lord, you need no angel or saint in heaven nor person on earth to represent you before God. Jesus is your Mediator, Advocate (1 John 2:1–2), and High Priest, interceding for you at the throne of God (Heb. 4:14–16). Just as the sun is sufficient to give light to our planet, so Jesus is sufficient to enlighten His church.

The sun is in the center of the earth's solar system and our planet orbits around it. Jesus is at the center of all things that relate to the Father and to His church and we must keep Him central. He must never be relegated to the fringes. The apostle John saw Jesus among the seven churches on earth (Rev. 1:13) and also in "the center before the throne" in heaven (Rev. 5:6; 7:17). When He was here on earth, Jesus was in the midst of the teachers in the temple (Luke 2:46), and He promises to be in the midst of His people when they assemble in His name (Matt. 18:20). At His crucifixion, He was placed between two thieves, accessible to both, and after His resurrection, He appeared in the midst of His disciples (Luke 24:36; John 20:19, 26). Jesus in the midst!

But why was Jesus Christ depicted at the center of things? To remind us "that in all things He may have the preeminence" (Col. 1:18 NKJV). It's unfortunate that there are people in our churches who are like Diotrephes and love to have the preeminence (3 John 9 NKJV).

During my many years of itinerant ministry, I preached to more than one church congregation that was divided and almost destroyed by people who wanted to be important and have their own way. We shouldn't be surprised if some Christians promote themselves; after all, even the apostles argued over which of them was the greatest (Luke 9:46; 22:24). But Jesus warned them, "For those who exalt themselves will be humbled, and those who humble themselves will be exalted" (Matt. 23:12).

If the sun were extinguished, life as we know it on the earth would also be extinguished. Jesus is "the light of life," but only to those who trust Him and follow Him. Yes, the Father "causes his sun to rise on the evil and the good" (Matt. 5:45), but the Son of God shines His grace and glory only on those who trust and obey. "But if we walk in the light, as he is in the light, we have fellowship with one another, and the blood of Jesus, his Son, purifies us from all sin" (1 John 1:7).

When we fellowship with the Lord, meditate on the Word, and obey what He commands, God's light shines "in our hearts to give us the light of the knowledge of God's glory displayed in the face of Christ" (2 Cor. 4:6). We not only learn more about Christ, but we also *become* more like Christ, "transformed into his image with ever-increasing glory, which comes from the Lord, who is the Spirit" (2 Cor. 3:18). The most important part of our lives is the part that only God sees—our daily worship time with Him; and to ignore that privilege or treat it carelessly will cause us gradually to go from heavenly sunshine into earthly shadows.

The nation of Israel was chosen to be "a light for the Gentiles" (Isa. 42:6; 49:6), a privilege that God eventually gave to Paul and the church (Acts 13:47). Jesus watched as the Jewish religious leaders lit the festal lamps each night, but the light did not transform anybody. They were just as blind as ever. The Jews may have boasted over Isaiah 42:6 (see Rom. 2:17–24), but they ignored Isaiah 42:7: "To open eyes that are blind, to free captives from prison and to release from the dungeon those who sit in darkness."

But that's exactly what Jesus did in John 9, and He is still doing it today through His faithful servants. Let's watch Him and learn how to do it.

The Living

James Hudson Taylor was weary and ill and had gone to visit friends in Brighton, England, where he hoped to find rest and spiritual enrichment. It was Sunday, June 25, 1865, and he had accompanied his friends to the morning worship service; but Taylor was "unable to bear the sight of rejoicing multitudes in the house of God."[2] He left the meeting and walked down to the seashore, his heart greatly burdened. How could so many believers be so joyful and yet do so very little to share that joy with the lost, especially the lost in China? On that Sunday morning, Hudson Taylor resolved that, with the Lord's help, he would begin a mission to reach the lost of inland China. Two days later, he went to the London and County Bank and with a ten-pound note opened an account in the name of the China Inland Mission.

That piece of Christian history reminds me of what Jesus did, as recorded at the end of John 8. It was the last day of the weeklong Festival of Booths and the people were celebrating in the temple. At the same time, their religious leaders were rejecting their own Messiah, who was standing among them; in fact, they were on the verge of stoning Him! Undisturbed, Jesus calmly departed from the temple area *and obeyed Isaiah 42:7 by bringing light to a blind beggar:* "To open eyes that are blind, to free captives from prison and to release from the dungeon those who sit in darkness."

Jesus is not visibly walking our city streets today, but His people are here to represent Him and spread the light. Millions of people profess to be followers of the Lord, so there ought to be plenty of light in this world; yet things seem to be getting darker. Jesus promises that if we follow Him, we will walk in the light, not in the darkness, and that His light will give us life. Even more, we will *be* lights in this dark world and help others find the true Light. "You are the light of the world," said Jesus. "A city on a hill cannot be hidden. Neither do people light a lamp and put it under a bowl. Instead they put it on its stand, and it gives light to everyone in the house. In the same way, let your light shine before others, that they may see your good deeds and glorify your Father in heaven" (Matt. 5:14–16). Paul put it like this: "For you were once darkness, but now you are light in the Lord. Live as children of light" (Eph. 5:8).

The festive crowd in the temple did not impress Jesus, nor did the angry religious leaders who wanted to kill Him disturb Him. He simply moved away from the crowd and went to help an individual

who was desperately in need. He left people who were spiritually
blind to go heal a man who was physically blind. Our Lord turned
away from the religious leaders who rejected Him and ministered
to a poor man who obeyed Him and ended up worshipping Him!
In the temple, Jesus exposed darkness and was rejected, but to the
beggar, He brought light and was worshipped. More than once the
record tells us that Jesus turned from the crowd in order to minister
to individuals, a practice that would bother believers today who mea-
sure ministry only by numbers.

How we look at other people determines how much we can
help them. To our Lord's disciples, the blind beggar was a theo-
logical problem to discuss and not a needy person to help. Perhaps
they had been discussing whether the beggar was even worthy of
help; for if his parents were the guilty ones, then the man couldn't
be blamed for his blindness. But Jesus totally rejected their view-
point and focused on the man and his needs. The next time you
sing "Jesus, the Very Thought of Thee," remember that the author,
Bernard of Clairvaux, said, "Justice seeks out the merits of the case,
but pity only regards the need." The disciples wanted justice; Jesus
opted for mercy.

Suppose that back in 1945, Jesus had asked me if I deserved to
be saved. Of course I didn't deserve it. I didn't deserve it then, and I
haven't deserved it since! I trusted Him, and in His mercy He didn't
give me what I did deserve: judgment. And in His grace He gave
me what I didn't deserve: salvation! "For he has rescued us from the
dominion of darkness and brought us into the kingdom of the Son
he loves, in whom we have redemption, the forgiveness of sins" (Col.
1:13–14). Christ is our Light and we trust Him; He is our Leader

and we follow Him; He is our Life and we grow in Him and reveal Him to this dark world.

The religious leaders and most of the common people in Jesus' day were blind to who He was and to the very Scriptures they claimed to obey. Jesus told them, "You study the Scriptures diligently because you think that in them you possess eternal life. These are the very Scriptures that testify about me, yet you refuse to come to me to have life" (John 5:39–40). When we trust Jesus and follow Him, He enables us to *see things as they really are.* The Jews bragged about their temple, but Jesus knew that the day would come when the Romans would destroy Herod's temple. The Jews also boasted of their great ancestor Abraham, but Jesus said that the first birth was not sufficient, and that people needed to be born again (John 3). The Jews and their Samaritan neighbors debated over whether Jerusalem or Mount Gerizim was God's appointed place for worship, and Jesus told them to forget geography and worship God "in the Spirit and in truth" (John 4:24). The priests poured out water at the Festival of Booths without realizing that the water represented the promised Holy Spirit (John 7:37–39).

David put it beautifully when he wrote, "For with you is the fountain of life; in your light we see light" (Ps. 36:9). We cannot receive light from history, science, or any other discipline unless God's light shines on it first. God's Word is light (Ps. 119:105, 130) and God's Spirit is light (Rev. 4:5), and if we yield to the Spirit and live in the Word, God will teach us. Apart from the Spirit's ministry, the Bible is a closed book. Furthermore, when we follow Jesus and walk in the light, we see this world and its dangerous illusions as they really are and we will not be deceived. "But you have an anointing from the Holy One, and all of you know the truth" (1 John 2:20).

Jesus told the Jews, "Then you will know the truth, and the truth will set you free" (John 8:32), but they didn't understand what He was saying. Because they had rejected the light, they thought He was talking about political freedom from slavery when He was actually referring to spiritual freedom from sin.

The way Jesus healed the blind beggar helps us better understand how we, the "children of light" (1 Thess. 5:5), may share God's love and be used by Him to open the eyes of those who are spiritually blind. First, Jesus put mud in the blind man's eyes, which must have seemed cruel to those who were watching; but Jesus knew what He was doing. He could heal blind eyes merely by touching them (Matt. 9:27–31) or by putting His spittle on them (Mark 8:22–26), but the irritation from the mud encouraged this man to obey our Lord's words: "Go wash in the Pool of Siloam" (John 9:7). As we witness to the lost, we must not fail to deal with sin, because there can be no conversion without conviction and contrition. The apostle John explains to his Gentile readers that "Siloam" means "sent" (v. 7), and he sees this as a reference to the Messiah, who was sent by the Father (see also 3:17, 34; 5:36; 7:29; 8:18, 42; 9:4). The beggar was healed by Jesus, not by the water from the Pool of Siloam.

Knowing it would anger the Pharisees, Jesus had deliberately healed the man on the Sabbath day, and this ignited a controversy. In their attempt to gather evidence against Jesus, the religious leaders interrogated the beggar and his parents, and four times they asked how he had been healed (John 9:10, 15, 19, 26). The parents were evasive, because they didn't want to be excommunicated from the synagogue; but the healed man did not change his testimony. In fact, his witness became so personal and powerful that the angry Pharisees insulted him and expelled him from the synagogue. This was a costly experience for a Jew, for it would cut him off from official worship and social fellowship. But better that he could see and build his own life than that he remain a blind beggar for the rest of his life. And Jesus always cares for His sheep. He found the man in the temple and there opened his spiritual eyes (Eph. 1:18) and brought him into the flock of the Lord (John 9:35–38).

It's beautiful to see how this man grew in his knowledge of who Jesus was. "The man they call Jesus" (John 9:11) was his first statement about Jesus, but then he said, "He is a prophet" (v. 17). The Pharisees called Jesus a sinner, for after all He had dishonored the Sabbath; but the beggar called Him a man of God (v. 33). When Jesus met him in the temple, the beggar discovered that this "sinner" was actually the Son of Man, a title of the Messiah (vv. 35–38; see also Dan. 7:13–14), and he worshipped Him. We will one day meet this healed man in heaven and hear from his own lips what the Savior did for him.

Did you notice how Jesus moved from the universal ("the light of the world") to the individual ("the one following me," see John 8:12)? That's because He brings His light to the world *through the good works of His own disciples.* James Hudson Taylor and his associates were lights shining in China, just as you and I must be lights shining wherever God has put us. The phrase "good works" includes many things, from visiting the lonely and feeding the hungry to teaching the ignorant, assisting the needy, and encouraging the discouraged. It always includes sharing the good news of Jesus and seeking to love others as Jesus loves us.

In our modern world, we are so accustomed to electric lights of all kinds that we forget the spiritual darkness that enshrouds our globe and blinds the minds and hearts of lost people. But the greatest tragedy is that people think they are "enlightened" when *the light that is in them is actually darkness.* Jesus said, "Your eye is the lamp of your body. When your eyes are healthy, your whole body also is full of light. But when they are unhealthy, your body also is full of darkness. See to it, then, that the light within you is not darkness" (Luke 11:34–35; see also John 9:39–41). Our outlook helps to determine our character and conduct; and character and conduct determine the outcome of life. To obey Jesus and follow the Light of the World means to become a living light and avoid the delusions that lead to the detours toward darkness. It means to become the kind of people who can point others to the Savior so that they too might experience "the light of life."

5

THE DOOR

Truly, truly, I say to you, he who does not enter by the door[1] into the fold of the sheep, but climbs up some other way, he is a thief and a robber. But he who enters by the door is a shepherd of the sheep. To him the doorkeeper opens, and the sheep hear his voice, and he calls his own sheep by name and leads them out.... Truly, truly, I say to you, I am the door of the sheep.... I am the door; if anyone enters through Me, he will be saved, and will go in and out and find pasture.

—John 10:1–3, 7, 9 NASB

The next day John [the Baptist] saw Jesus coming toward him and said, "Look, the Lamb of God, who takes away the sin of the world! ... I myself did not know him, but the reason I

came baptizing with water was that he might be
revealed to Israel."

—**John 1:29, 31**

The images of the shepherd and the door to the sheepfold are woven
together in John 10, because both refer to Jesus. This explains how
Jesus can be the door into the fold when He also enters the fold
and leads the sheep out of the fold (vv. 2–5, 9). In the language of
metaphor, a blending of images is not unusual. For example, Jesus *is*
the bread of life (John 6:35), and yet He *gives* the bread (Himself)
to hungry sinners. He speaks the truth (8:45), but He also *is* the
truth (14:6). He imparts life to believing sinners (6:50–51), and yet
He *is* life (14:6). Jesus Himself is the incarnation of every spiritual
blessing He wants to give us, for "in Christ you have been brought
to fullness" (Col. 2:10).

If we were to view John 10 as a drama, the program might look
like this:

Cast of Characters

Director: God the Father (mentioned thirteen times in
John 10)

The Door and the Good Shepherd: Jesus Christ, the Son of
God

The False Shepherds: Thieves, robbers, hirelings, strangers
(religious leaders who opposed Jesus)

The Sheep: True believers, Jews, and Gentiles

The Gatekeeper (or Porter): John the Baptist

Time and Place

John 10:1–21: The temple in Jerusalem after the celebration of the Festival of Booths and the healing of the blind beggar

John 10:22–39: The temple in Jerusalem during the Festival of Dedication, two and a half months after the events recorded in John 9:1—10:21

Act I	John 10:1–10	Jesus the Door
Act II	John 10:11–21	Jesus the Good Shepherd
Act III	John 10:22–39	Jesus and the True Sheep

For the people of Israel, the Festival of Dedication (Hanukkah)[2] commemorates the rededication of the temple in 165 BC. The Syrian invaders had defiled it, and the Jewish priests reconsecrated it. The festival lasts eight days and is celebrated in December, around the same time as the

**Christian Christmas. It is also called the
Festival of Lights. Each celebrating Jewish
family has a special eight-branched[3] oil
lamp or candlestick, called a menorah. A
new lamp or candle is lit on each day of the
festival until all eight are burning. In this
way the family is reminded that the light of
God's truth returned to their temple so that
the people might worship Jehovah once
more.**

The Jewish people have always seen their nation as the flock of
Jehovah, cared for by the Lord, their Shepherd (Num. 27:15–17;
2 Sam. 24:17; Ps. 23:1; 74:1; 77:20; 78:52; 79:13; 80:1; 100:3;
Jer. 23:1–4; Ezek. 34; Matt. 15:24). The image of the flock is also
applied to the church (Luke 12:32; Acts 20:28–29; Rom. 8:36; Heb.
13:20–21; 1 Peter 5:2–3), and spiritual leaders are known as "pastors" (Eph. 4:11), from the Latin word for *shepherd.*

Let's consider first the physical aspects of the sheepfold, and
then we will better understand the spiritual lessons Jesus wants
to convey to us. The sheepfold was an enclosure surrounded by
a wall of rocks that was too high for the sheep to jump over. The
shepherds sometimes put thorny branches on the tops of the walls
to deter thieves from trying to climb over. An opening in the wall
allowed the sheep to enter and exit; and at night, the shepherd lay
across that opening and became the door of the sheepfold. No animal could get out and no enemy could get in without the shepherd
knowing it. On the outskirts of many villages there might be a

community sheepfold where all the shepherds brought their flocks each evening. In the morning, the shepherds would call their sheep, and each flock would follow its shepherd out of the sheepfold. The sheep knew the voice of their own shepherd and would follow nobody else.

Knowing these facts, we can now meditate on Jesus Christ as the Door and learn what this truth means to us today. In the next chapter we will consider Jesus Christ the Good Shepherd.

The Door Means Separation

We are so accustomed to modern, attractive doors, some of which open and close automatically, that we don't get too excited about a mere opening in a wall; but that opening was very efficient for the shepherds. During the day, when the flock was grazing, the shepherd could easily watch for danger; but at night, the sheep had to be together and behind safe walls, with the shepherd serving as the door. At night, the flock separated from darkness by that door is the safe flock.

I believe that two sheepfolds are involved in John 10:1–10: the Jewish fold, out of which Jesus led those who believed in Him (vv. 1–6); and the believers' fold, into which Jesus led both Jews and Gentiles and permits them to go in and out and enjoy their new life of freedom (vv. 7–10). Jesus came as Israel's Messiah in exactly the way the Scriptures had promised. He was the seed of a Jewish woman, a descendant of Abraham (Gen. 3:15; 12:3), born of a virgin (Isa. 7:14), born in Bethlehem of the tribe of Judah (Mic. 5:2; Gen. 49:10), and of the house of David (2 Sam. 7:12–13). He would be of humble birth but anointed by the Spirit (Isa. 11:1–2). A forerunner would precede Him (Isa. 40:3; Mal. 3:1). By the time Jesus came to the Jordan to be baptized and presented to the nation by John the Baptist, all these elements of His credentials could be known (John 1:19–34).

Jesus was born into the Jewish fold (Gal. 4:4–5), and during His earthly ministry He called His sheep out of Judaism and into the Christian fold. Before they left on their first ministry trip, the disciples were told, "Do not go among the Gentiles or enter any town of the Samaritans. Go rather to the lost sheep of Israel" (Matt. 10:5–6). But Jesus made it clear that He would also call the Gentiles ("other sheep," John 10:16; see also John 11:49–52; 12:32). Over the centuries, our Lord has been calling sinners out of whatever fold they were in and putting them into the freedom of His "one flock" over which He is the "one shepherd" (John 10:16). We will have more to say about this in the next chapter when we consider Jesus the Good Shepherd.

This matter of "calling out" people brings to mind the experience of the blind beggar recorded in John 9. He had been born into the Jewish fold, but the religious leaders excommunicated him from the synagogue—"they threw him out" (v. 34)—because he honored Jesus. But Jesus found him in the temple, led him to saving faith, and brought him into His own flock. Jesus has nobody's "sheep" in His flock but His own, those who trust Him, hear His voice (the Word), and follow Him no matter the cost.

For example, Saul of Tarsus was "a Hebrew of Hebrews" (Phil. 3:5), but Jesus called him out of the Jewish fold and into the Christian flock; and Paul the apostle proved his faith by "coming in and going out" with Christ's flock in Jerusalem (see Acts 9:28). He abandoned everything for membership in Christ's flock (Phil. 3). He was the leading young Jewish zealot of his day (Gal. 1:13–14), yet he forsook all of that to become "Paul, the apostle of Jesus Christ." The name *Paul* means "little" in Latin. Paul said with John the Baptist, "He [Jesus] must become greater; I must become less" (John 3:30).

A door creates a division: Some people are outside and some are inside. "Thus the people were divided because of Jesus" (John 7:43). "So they were divided" (9:16). "The Jews who heard these words were again divided" (10:19). At our Lord's birth, the angels announced peace on earth (Luke 2:14), but as He moved toward the cross, Jesus said to His disciples, "Do you think I came to bring peace on earth? No, I tell you, but division. From now on there will be five in one family divided against each other, three against two and two against three" (Luke 12:51–52). Those who follow Christ don't belong to this world, nor do they live like the world, and this causes the people of the world to hate them (John 16:18–25).

In my pastoral ministry, I don't know how many times the congregation and I have prayed for and stood with people who trusted Christ and were rejected by their families and friends. These new believers dared to leave the "old fold" and by faith enter the "one flock" of the Good Shepherd. It was a costly step, *but not to have made it would have been much more costly!* "If the world hates you," said Jesus, "keep in mind that it hated me first. If you belonged to the world, it would love you as its own" (John 15:18–19). When the world treats us the way it treated Jesus, it's really a compliment, because it means we are sharing in "the fellowship of His sufferings" (Phil. 3:10 NASB).

The Door Means Decision

We live in a world that promotes tolerance at the cost of truth. "What's true for you may not be true for me," people argue; but if you were talking about money, medicine, or measurements, that statement would never stand. When it comes to money, medicine, and measurements, there are absolutes that must not be denied.

If a friend owed you a hundred dollars and tried to pay you with ten one-dollar bills, would you accept that payment? If he argued that, in his opinion, a one-dollar bill was the same as a ten-dollar bill, would you agree? Or, suppose your pharmacist used arsenic instead of aspirin in your prescription, would you swallow the medicine? If a carpenter built you a bookcase ten inches wide and eight inches tall, instead of ten feet wide and eight feet tall, and argued that an inch is as good as a foot, would you pay him for his work? *If we want absolutes in matters that concern measurement, money, and medicine, why not in matters of personal morality and faith?*

I try to be tolerant of other people's opinions, *but not when they deny absolutes.* Plastic words and plastic ideas that can be molded to please everybody are very dangerous, and I will not accept them. In 2 Peter 2:1–3, Peter warns us against false teachers who try to exploit us "with fabricated stories." The word *fabricated* is the translation of the Greek word *plastos* from which we get our English word *plastic.* What are plastic words? They are words that can be molded and twisted to mean almost anything. False teachers may use what appears to be a Christian vocabulary, *but they do not use a Christian dictionary!* Same words, different meanings. These false teachers do not believe in absolutes, and therefore they are dangerous.

When we come to Jesus the Door, we must hear His Word, accept it as truth, and act upon it. When I hear somebody say, "Well, what do you mean by sin?" or "Aren't there many roads to heaven?" I know I'm dealing with a master of "plastic words." Jesus prayed to the Father, "Sanctify them [His followers] by the truth; your word is truth" (John 17:17). Proverbs 23:23 warns, "Buy the truth and do not sell it." There is such a thing as *the truth,* and no amount of plastic words can replace it.

Years ago, people used to sing this children's chorus in Sunday school:

> One door and only one, and yet its sides are two.
> Inside and outside—on which side are you?
> One door and only one, and yet its sides are two.
> I'm on the inside—on which side are you?

To stand before Jesus Christ, the Door, and make no decision at all is to *stay on the outside of salvation!* It means not entering the "one flock" of which Jesus is the Savior and the Good Shepherd. At the door you are in a place of decision, and to make no decision is to make a decision—the wrong one.

The Door Means Salvation

Salvation is not a human right but a gift of God's grace; however, what Jesus says in John 10:9 reminds me of what Thomas Jefferson wrote in the American Declaration of Independence:

> We hold these truths to be self-evident, that all
> men are created equal, that they are endowed by

their Creator with certain unalienable rights, that among these are life, liberty, and the pursuit of happiness.

Salvation means life. Here is our Lord's promise: "Whoever enters through me will be saved" (John 10:9). We are not saved because we admire Jesus but because we repent of our sins and trust Him and Him alone as our Lord and Savior. The beggar in John 9 wasn't saved by going to the temple but by meeting Jesus in the temple, bowing before Him, and saying, "Lord, I believe" (John 9:35–38).

To be saved means to have your sins forgiven, to become a child of God, and to have the assurance of heaven. It means to have eternal life (John 3:16–18) and "life to the full" (10:10). "Whoever believes in the Son has eternal life, but whoever rejects the Son will not see life, for God's wrath remains on them" (3:36). Any sinner who enters into the one flock through Jesus Christ is saved and always will be saved. "My sheep listen to my voice; I know them, and they follow me. I give them eternal life, and they shall never perish; no one will snatch them out of my hand" (10:27–28).

Salvation means liberty. Salvation brings to us eternal life, but it also gives us the privilege of enjoying liberty—"they will go in and out...." Jesus leads us out of the old fold and into the new flock, and then He permits us to go in and out of the walled community because of the freedom we have in Him. Jesus said that "everyone who sins is a slave to sin.... So if the Son sets you free, you will be free indeed" (John 8:34, 36). Christian freedom doesn't mean the right to do whatever we please; it means we have the privilege of following Christ and doing what pleases Him. True freedom is life controlled by truth and motivated by love.

Note the balance here: "in and out." A timid, frightened sheep would stay in the fold day and night and never see the pastures chosen by the shepherd, but the careless, overconfident sheep would remain in the pastures day and night and be exposed to all kinds of dangers. We need the food, water, and exercise of the pasture as well as the rest and security of the fold. Prayer and meditation are important, but so are witness and service, which is why the book of Hebrews tells us to go "within the veil" to worship the Lord and then to go "outside the camp" to work and witness for the Lord (Heb. 6:19; 13:13 NASB). Blessed are the balanced!

Out in the pasture, the sheep have no walls and are free to move about, while in the fold they are confined; and both are needed in the Christian life. There are some areas of life that require walls and fences, and if we ignore them, we get into trouble. There are other areas of Christian life that are open and free and about which the saints may even disagree. Paul's wise counsel is, "Everyone should be fully convinced in their own mind" (Rom. 14:5). Not prejudice, tradition, or opinion, but full conviction is the mark of maturity, decisions based on the Word of God and witnessed by the Spirit of God. "You, my brothers and sisters, were called to be free. But do not use your freedom to indulge the sinful nature; rather, serve one another humbly in love" (Gal. 5:13).

When you walk into some church sanctuaries, you see a sign over the entrance that reads "Enter to worship." When you walk out after the service, the sign reads "Depart to serve." It's a reminder for us to cultivate a balanced life. Our zeal must be balanced with knowledge and our love with discernment (Phil. 1:9). Fellowship should be balanced with solitude (Matt. 6:5–6), and private prayer balanced with public prayer that involves other believers.

Salvation means the pursuit of happiness. Note the plural: "pastures." Perhaps the older sheep prefer to graze in familiar territory where they know the terrain, while the lambs feel better frisking away into new places, not even caring what the shepherd has planned. Both are incomplete. The shepherd always knows what is best for his flock: "The LORD is my shepherd, I lack nothing. He makes me lie down in green pastures, he leads me beside quiet waters, he refreshes my soul. He guides me along the right paths for his name's sake" (Ps. 23:1–3).

In my many years of following the Shepherd, I have learned that I need new discoveries of His grace and guidance as well as experiences in the old paths and pastures. The Hebrew word for *paths* in Psalm 23:3 means "deep ruts." These paths are so important and necessary that many others have walked in them and created these ruts for us. "Ask for the ancient paths," said Jeremiah, "ask where the good way is, and walk in it, and you will find rest for your souls" (Jer. 6:16).

When it comes to the basics of the life of faith, Solomon tells us "there is nothing new under the sun" (Eccl. 1:9). But we need new challenges if we are to mature in our Christian walks, challenges that older saints have already encountered. Old paths and new opportunities go together. As we follow the Lord into the pastures He has chosen for us, we experience the joy of the Lord, even in the midst of trials. We'll discover more about this when we focus on the Shepherd in the next chapter.

Life, liberty, and the pursuit of happiness are what we experience when we let Jesus the Shepherd lead us in and out of the sheepfold day after day.

The Door Means Compassion

In the evening, when the shepherd had led his flock back to the fold, he stood at the door, gave them a cool drink of water ("my cup overflows," Ps. 23:5), and inspected each animal as it passed under his crook. A faithful shepherd was a "physician" as well as a guide and protector, and if a sheep had a serious bruise or laceration, the shepherd would apply medication. "You anoint my head with oil" (v. 5) describes this ministry. The shepherd would also remove any burs or thorns that had been picked up during the day. Was any animal limping? The shepherd would detect it and seek to find out the cause. Was one of the sheep missing? The shepherd would make certain the flock was safe, enlist another shepherd to be the door, and search for the missing sheep.

In other words, the shepherd was concerned about the welfare of individual sheep as well as the general condition of the whole flock. One sheep or lamb was important to him. He used soothing oil on wounds; oil in Scripture is one of the symbols of the Holy Spirit (Ex. 30:22–33). When our Good Shepherd wants to comfort and encourage us, it is through the ministry of the Holy Spirit, for each believer has received the anointing of God's Spirit (2 Cor. 1:21; 1 John 2:20, 27). The shepherd would give each sheep a satisfying drink of cool water, another symbol of the Spirit (John 7:37–39).

It continues to impress me how Jesus always had time for individuals, whether an unclean leper, a Roman soldier, a Samaritan woman, a perplexed Pharisee, or a dying thief; and He is just as concerned today as He was yesterday. His under-shepherds need to imitate Him and take care of the individual needs of the sheep. In our pulpit ministries, we can teach, warn, and encourage the entire flock; but it takes personal ministry to discover the hidden needs and remedy them.

I have had enough pastoral experience to know that almost every church has its share of "problem people" as well as "people with problems." Many people with personal problems don't want to share them with others, especially their busy pastoral staff, while "problem people" get attention and sympathy by telling as many people as possible all that they are enduring. They don't really want to solve their problems; if they did, they would lose their identity and importance! They schedule frequent meetings with the pastor, who patiently listens to the same stories he has heard many times over. He knows that honest confrontation will not bring about any changes, because these people hear only what they want to hear and interpret it their own way.

In spite of these difficulties, shepherds need to take a personal interest in their people and invest the time necessary for uncovering problems and offering solutions. Pastoral preaching is effective when the listeners detect in the preacher's manner a loving concern, an understanding heart, and a biblical approach to solving the problem. The prophet Ezekiel was writing about selfish civil rulers in 34:11–16, but the application to the shepherd of the church flock is perfectly legitimate. God wants His shepherds to search for the lost sheep (v. 11), rescue those in danger (v. 12), bring them out of their bondage (v. 13), bring them back into the fellowship of the flock (v. 13), and care for them (vv. 13–16).

I recall hearing that one of our men in the church had walked out on his wife and family and nobody knew where he was. I asked the Lord to bring us together as if by accident so I could chat with him, *and He did!* I walked into a restaurant to get some lunch, looked at a booth, and there he was! "Got room for another hungry man?" I asked, and he graciously asked me to join him. An hour later we were praying together. He said he would go home and make things right; and he did, and he came back to church.

The gifted American preacher George W. Truett was frequently approached to leave his Dallas pulpit and become a full-time denominational leader, a college or university president, or an itinerant evangelist, and his reply was always the same: "I have sought and found a pastor's heart." No wonder he stayed at Dallas First Baptist Church forty-seven years!

The Door Means Protection

The shepherd risked his own life (and probably lost some sleep) when he served as the door of the sheepfold. The wolves could not get in and attack the sheep, nor could thieves enter and steal from the flock. The shepherd was armed with his rod and staff and could fend off intruders (Ps. 23:4).

Wherever there is a faithful flock, there will be enemies waiting to attack, from outside the church or from within. Paul made
that clear in his farewell address to the Ephesian elders, a passage all
shepherds need written on their hearts.

> Keep watch over yourselves and all the flock of
> which the Holy Spirit has made you overseers. Be
> shepherds of the church of God, which he bought
> with his own blood. I know that after I leave, sav-
> age wolves will come in among you and will not
> spare the flock. Even from your own number some
> will arise and distort the truth in order to draw
> away disciples after them. So be on your guard!
> Remember that for three years I never stopped
> warning each of you night and day with tears.
> (Acts 20:28–31)

The security of the flock is the shepherd's number one responsibility, and Jesus assures us that His sheep shall never perish (John
10:27–30). "Therefore he is able to save completely [forever] those
who come to God through him, because he always lives to intercede
for them" (Heb. 7:25). We are saved as long as Jesus is alive in heaven,
and "Jesus lives forever" (v. 24). Jesus, our heavenly High Priest, min-
isters for us today "on the basis of the power of an indestructible life"
(v. 16). No wonder He could say to His disciples, "Because I live, you
also will live" (John 14:19).

In our next study of John 10, we will seek to get to know this
Shepherd better.

6

THE GOOD SHEPHERD

I am the good shepherd. The good shepherd lays down his life for the sheep. The hired hand is not the shepherd and does not own the sheep. So when he sees the wolf coming, he abandons the sheep and runs away. Then the wolf attacks the flock and scatters it. The man runs away because he is a hired hand and cares nothing for the sheep. I am the good shepherd; I know my sheep and my sheep know me—just as the Father knows me and I know the Father—and I lay down my life for the sheep. I have other sheep that are not of this sheep pen. I must bring them also. They too will listen to my voice, and there shall be one flock and one shepherd.

—John 10:11–16

My sheep listen to my voice; I know them, and they follow me. I give them eternal life, and they

shall never perish; no one will snatch them out of
my hand. My Father, who has given them to me, is
greater than all; no one can snatch them out of my
Father's hand. I and the Father are one.

—John 10:27–30

The LORD is my shepherd, I lack nothing.

—Psalm 23:1

Know that the LORD is God. It is he who made us, and
we are his; we are his people, the sheep of his pasture.

—Psalm 100:3

We all, like sheep, have gone astray, each of us has
turned to our own way; and the LORD has laid on
him the iniquity of us all.

—Isaiah 53:6

For the Lamb at the center before the throne will
be their shepherd; "he will lead them to springs of
living water." "And God will wipe away every tear
from their eyes."

—Revelation 7:17

Some well-meaning people want to remove the shepherd-and-sheep image from Scripture, but if we did, we would rob ourselves of several great leaders as well as a great deal of nourishing spiritual truth. "After all," they argue, "most people in our churches live in cities and have never even seen shepherds and sheep." But if God's servants are limited to preaching and teaching only that which is already familiar to people, none of us will ever learn very much.

It's doubtful that anyone in our churches has ever seen a crucifixion or a resurrection, but if you eliminate these events, you can't preach the gospel. How many professed Christians can confidently say they have seen an angel or a miracle or, for that matter, the Lord Jesus Christ? It's obvious that this "never seen" approach to God's Word is not only dangerous but also ridiculous. All Scripture is inspired and profitable, and that includes the shepherds and the sheep.

Paul used the shepherd image when he admonished the Ephesian elders, and Ephesus was a large city (Acts 20:28). The apostle John used the words *shepherd, sheep,* and especially *lamb* (over thirty references) when writing to churches in seven key cities in Asia Minor. Eliminate these images from your Bible and you will have no Savior, no gospel, and not much hope.

Jesus calls Himself "the Good Shepherd" because He is the genuine shepherd in contrast to the false shepherds and hired hands who over the centuries had exploited God's people. Remember that civil rulers such as kings, princes, and governors were called shepherds, even though many of them were more like wolves and robbers (Isa. 56:9–12; Ezek. 34). The promised Messiah was to be a loving shepherd (Isa. 40:9–11; Ezek. 34:20–24), and Jesus is that Messiah. The word translated "good" in "good shepherd" carries the meanings of "noble, praiseworthy, desirable, and pleasing to God." Jesus qualifies.

Sheep are mentioned in the Bible over three hundred times, more than any other animal. It may be embarrassing to some believers to learn that sheep are defenseless animals and prone to go astray. (They have poor eyesight and tend to follow other sheep without thinking.) Sheep can also be very stubborn. They are ceremonially clean animals and were frequently offered for sacrifices. The Jewish people raised sheep primarily for the wool, milk, and lambs, and they slaughtered sheep for food only on special festive occasions.

During my many years of ministry, I have pastored three "flocks" and have been a member of three different churches while I was serving in parachurch ministries. I have preached in hundreds of churches and counseled with pastors in many parts of the world; so for over sixty years I have been taking care of sheep and studying them from several different perspectives. However, the sheep mean nothing apart from Jesus Christ, the Good Shepherd. Let's examine the relationships that exist between Jesus the Good Shepherd and His sheep, and let's apply these truths to our own lives as members of His flock.

The Shepherd Owns the Sheep

Christ's sheep are called "his own sheep" (John 10:3–4) and "my sheep" (vv. 14, 26–27) because He claims them as His flock. They are His because the Father gave them to Him (v. 29; see also John 17:2, 6, 9, 24) and because He purchased them when He died on the cross (10:11, 15, 17–18; see also 13:37–38; 1 John 3:16). "Greater

love has no one than this: to lay down one's life for one's friends"
(John 15:13). But Jesus laid down His life for rebellious sinners who
were His enemies (Rom. 5:6–10)! "You are not your own; you were
bought at a price" (1 Cor. 6:19–20).

Our Lord's death is mentioned several times in John's gospel,
and each text reveals something special about that death. He died
sacrificially: "Look, the Lamb of God, who takes away the sin of
the world!" (1:29). Under the old covenant, the sheep died for the
shepherds; but under the new covenant, the shepherd died for the
sheep. Who but God knows how many lambs were sacrificed during
Israel's national history? But Jesus in one act of sacrifice died for the
sins of the whole world, once and for all!

He died *brutally,* like a building torn down and left in ruins
(John 2:18–22). Crucifixion was the most barbaric form of execu-
tion, and Psalm 22:1–21 and Isaiah 52:14 give us some indication of
the price Jesus paid to save His sheep. Like the serpent lifted up on
the pole (Num. 21:4–9; John 3:14–15), Jesus was lifted up on the
cross and died *shamefully. Imagine the holy Son of God identifying with
a cursed serpent!*

But He died *willingly* (John 10:11–18). He laid down His life.
Would you be willing to give your life to rescue a sheep? What driver
would risk his life to keep from hitting a sheep on the highway? A
human is worth more than a sheep, yet Jesus loved us enough to die
for us.

He died *triumphantly* (John 12:20–29). The seed was planted
in the ground, and it produced a beautiful, bountiful harvest to the
glory of the Father. He laid down His life that He might take it
up again in glorious resurrection (10:17–18)! He did this for us so

that we might be *His* sheep and be able to say from our hearts, "My beloved is mine and I am his" (Song 2:16; see also 6:3).

Hired hands take care of the sheep primarily because they get paid for it, but they have no personal love for the flock. When wolves and thieves show up, hired hands run away and hide, and the enemies are free to ravage the flock. But Jesus owns us, and He proved His love by dying for us! We belong to Him and therefore ought to follow Him and do His will.

At a time in life when pioneer missionary C. T. Studd should have been planning for retirement, he was heading for Africa. When a newspaper reporter asked him why, he replied, "If Jesus Christ be God and died for me, then no sacrifice can be too great for me to make for Him."

Jesus owns His sheep. If they follow Him, they experience the abundant life He alone can give. "I have come that they may have life, and have it to the full" (John 10:10). If they don't follow Him, they forfeit life to the full and have only emptiness; and the Shepherd must discipline them, which is not a pleasant experience.

The Shepherd Knows His Sheep

"I am the good shepherd; I know my sheep and my sheep know me—just as the Father knows me and I know the Father" (John 10:14–15).

In Scripture, "to know" means much more than to be able to identify a person or a thing by name. In Bible language, "to know" involves intimacy, a deep understanding of the person or object involved. It means to be chosen, to be loved. In the original Hebrew text, the word *know* describes the intimate love between husband and wife. At the time of judgment, Jesus will say to those who masqueraded as believers, "I never knew you. Away from me, you evildoers!" (Matt. 7:23; see also 25:12).

Eastern shepherds knew the name of each sheep and could call it out of the fold each morning. But the shepherds also knew the nature of each sheep: those that were prone to wander, those that wanted their own way, those that delayed obeying their shepherd's commands. Because the shepherds possessed this kind of knowledge, they were better able to care for the flock.

But the sheep also knew their shepherd! Just as children come to understand their parents better and pupils their teachers, so sheep learn to "read" their shepherd's voice and gestures. They know when he is warning them, when he is calling them together, and when he is simply reminding them that he is watching.

For Jesus to compare His relationship with His sheep to His relationship with His Father is quite remarkable. It reminds me of what Jesus said to His Father when He concluded His prayer recorded in John 17: "I have made you known to them, and will continue to make you known in order that the love you have for me may be in them and that I myself may be in them" (v. 26). The Father loves us as much as He loves Jesus! The better we get to know Jesus and the Father, the more we will love God and experience His love in our hearts, and the better we will obey Him. The shepherds had a loving relationship with their sheep, the kind of relationship we should have with our Good Shepherd. As we study the Word, worship, fellowship, and obey the Shepherd, we come to know Him *and also ourselves* better.

It encourages me to know that my Shepherd knows and understands me thoroughly *and still loves me and cares for me.* "You have searched me, LORD, and you know me. You know when I sit and when I rise; you perceive my thoughts from afar. You discern my going out and my lying down; you are familiar with all my ways" (Ps. 139:1–3).

Albert Einstein's wife was asked if she understood Dr. Einstein's mathematical theories, and she replied, "No, but I understand Dr. Einstein."

The apostle Paul had been saved for thirty years, had been to heaven and back, and had seen Christ in His glory, and yet he wrote, "I want to know Christ" (Phil. 3:10). He prayed that the Christians in Ephesus might "know him better" (Eph. 1:17), a prayer we should be praying daily.

The Shepherd Calls His Sheep

"He calls his own sheep by name and leads them out. When he has brought out all his own, he goes on ahead of them, and his sheep follow him because they know his voice. But they will never follow a stranger; in fact, they will run away from him because they do not recognize a stranger's voice" (John 10:3–5).

In his sermon on Pentecost, Peter said, "The promise [of salvation] is for you and your children and for all who are far off—for all whom the Lord our God will call" (Acts 2:39). Paul identified the people of God as "the called of Jesus Christ" (Rom. 1:6 NASB; see also 8:30; 9:24). The Lord calls sinners through the preaching of the gospel (2 Thess. 2:14). He calls us out of the darkness of unbelief and sin and into the light of His glory (1 Peter 2:9). He calls us out so that we may follow Him (John 10:4, 9, 28), and this means a change of mind and a complete separation from the old life, what the Scriptures call "repentance." There can be no compromise. Jesus said, "Whoever is not with me is against me, and whoever does not gather with me scatters" (Matt. 12:30). He wants disciples, not just converts.

God's call to us is totally an act of grace; we have done nothing to deserve it. For me to say, "He called me because He foreknew that I would believe" is to twist what the Scriptures say, because He foreknew us (elected us), and this is why He called us and we believed. "For those God foreknew [elected] he also predestined to be conformed to the image of his Son.... And those he predestined, he also called; those he called, he also justified; those he justified, he also glorified" (Rom. 8:29–30). Note our Lord's dramatic statement in John 10:26: "But you do not believe because you are not my sheep." He did not say, "You are not my sheep because you have not believed."

"He calls his own sheep by name" (John 10:3). He called Abraham by name (Gen. 22:1, 11), as well as Moses (Ex. 3:4), Samuel (1 Sam. 3:1–10), Simon (John 1:42; Luke 22:31), Martha (Luke 10:41), Zacchaeus (Luke 19:5), and Mary Magdalene (John 20:16). Today we don't hear God's voice as those believers did, but the Holy Spirit uses the Word of God to convince our minds and convict our hearts, and we cry out, "What shall we do?" (Acts 2:36–37). One mark of a true Christian is a "spiritual ear" that is sensitive to the Word of God. "Whoever has ears, let them hear" (Matt. 11:15).

As we witness to the lost, we don't know who God's elect are, nor should we worry ourselves about these eternal mysteries. Our commission is to share the gospel in the power of the Spirit and trust the Lord to call out those who are His. *If we did not know God has His "sheep" in this lost world, it would be hopelessly discouraging to tell the good news to anybody!* The Lord told Paul when he was ministering in Corinth, "Do not be afraid; keep on speaking, do not be silent. For I am with you, and no one is going to attack and harm you, because I have many people in this city" (Acts 18:9–10). Divine election is not a deterrent to evangelism but one of the dynamics behind evangelism.

Our Shepherd not only calls us out of whatever fold we were in and saves us, but He also calls us to follow Him into the things He wants us to do; and then we serve Him. Because our unsaved friends and relatives can't hear His voice, they think we are making a big mistake, but we have nothing to worry about. *Our Shepherd goes before us and prepares the way* (John 10:4). Whenever we unwittingly move out of His will, the Lord closes the doors until we wait long enough to hear His voice (Acts 16:6–10). As long as we are willing to do His will and daily hearing His voice in the Word and praying for guidance, He will never allow us to stray (John 7:17; Phil. 3:15–16).

The Holy Spirit within us warns us when we are listening to voices different from our Shepherd's. Dr. H. A. Ironside told about walking with a young believer in downtown Los Angeles and encountering a "street preacher." The young believer saw the man had a Bible, so he stopped to listen while Dr. Ironside walked on. He knew that the preacher was a cultist masquerading as an evangelical. In a few minutes, the young believer caught up with Dr.

Ironside, who asked him, "What did you think of the preacher?"
The young believer replied, "All the time I listened, my heart said,
'Liar! Liar!'"

The Shepherd Cares for His Sheep

The thief tries to steal the sheep secretly, the robber wants to exploit
the sheep violently, and the hired hand runs away fearfully when
the wolf appears; but the true shepherd cares for the flock lovingly
and courageously. He goes before them and finds the best pastures
and the safest sources of water, and he knows when the sheep must
lie down and rest. He makes sure there are no holes or dangerous
enemies hidden in the pasture, and he keeps his eyes on the sheep
that he knows are prone to go astray.

Bible students for centuries have pointed out that the Good
Shepherd is described in Psalm 22, laying down His life for the sheep
(vv. 1–21). The Chief Shepherd is pictured in Psalm 24, returning
and rewarding the faithful under-shepherds (1 Peter 5:1–4). But it's
in Psalm 23 that we see the Great Shepherd equipping and enabling
the sheep (Heb. 13:20–21). It's unfortunate that this marvelous
psalm is read primarily at funerals, because it describes our Lord's
loving ministry to His people all the days of our lives (Ps. 23:6).

King David wrote Psalm 23 out of his own experience as a shepherd as well as from the way God cared for him. "I lack nothing"
(v. 1). "I will fear no evil" (v. 4). "I will dwell in the house of the
LORD forever" (v. 6). Green pastures, quiet waters, right paths, dark
valleys, dangerous enemies—no circumstance is beyond the skill of
the Great Shepherd of the sheep. A true shepherd has a heart for

the sheep and seeks the very best for them. He protects them and provides for them, and he also corrects them when they want to have their own way. At the close of the day, when the shepherd leads the flock back to the fold, he examines each sheep for wounds or injuries and becomes a tender physician. He wants the sheep to be comfortable as they settle down for the night.

New Christians must learn early in their spiritual walks to allow the Shepherd to feed and refresh them from the Word of God. A lamb knows its mother and has a desire for her milk (1 Peter 2:2–3), but as the Lord's lamb matures in the Lord, it moves from nursing to eating solid food (Heb. 5:11—6:3). The Shepherd teaches His sheep how to feed themselves in the green pastures of the Scriptures, and they know just where to turn in the Bible to find the truth that they need. Unless each day we allow the Shepherd to feed us from the Word of God, we can never "grow in the grace and knowledge of our Lord and Savior Jesus Christ" (2 Peter 3:18).

Shepherds care for their sheep because they want each of them to mature and fulfill their purposes in God's natural order. Rams and ewes should reproduce and help their lambs to grow up, and lambs should in time mature, reproduce, and enlarge the flock. *If all of God's sheep would reproduce, and if all the lambs would mature and the flock would obey the Shepherd, how different churches would be!* Faithful shepherds can do only so much; the sheep should assume their responsibilities as well. "Therefore let us move beyond the elementary teachings about Christ and be taken forward to maturity" (Heb. 6:1). The Holy Spirit will take us forward if we will spend time daily in the Word and prayer and abandon "the ways of childhood" (1 Cor. 13:11).

But pastors and other local church spiritual leaders must also fulfill their ministries, and our Lord's words to Peter point the way (John 21:15–17): "Feed my lambs." "Take care of my sheep." "Feed my sheep." And the most important responsibility they have is *to love Jesus Christ more than anything else*. If we love Jesus Christ, we will love His sheep, and we will sacrifice to serve them. Remember, when we serve others in the name of Christ, we are serving Him (Matt. 25:40). "Keep watch over yourselves and all the flock of which the Holy Spirit has made you overseers. Be shepherds of the church of God, which he bought with his own blood" (Acts 20:28).

He Gathers His Flock

Jesus began His ministry going "to the lost sheep of Israel" (Matt. 10:5–6), but He made it clear that the Gentiles would be included in His church. "I have other sheep that are not of this sheep pen. I must bring them also. They too will listen to my voice, and there shall be one flock and one shepherd" (John 10:16). Note that He did not say "one fold," for there are still a Jewish fold and a Gentile fold in our world; but He spoke of "one flock," the church of Jesus Christ of which He is the one shepherd. Peter's message at Pentecost (Acts 2) was directed to Jews and Gentile proselytes to Judaism. But later, Peter went with John to Samaria, and the Lord took believing Samaritans into the flock (Acts 8:14–17). By the time we get to Acts 10, Peter is sent to the home of the Roman centurion Cornelius, a Gentile, and he and his relatives and close friends are saved and brought into the flock.

There is one flock and Jesus is the one shepherd. There is one body and Jesus is the head (Eph. 2:16; 3:6; 4:4, 25). There is one building and Jesus is the foundation (2:11–22). The Father's grand purpose is "to bring unity to all things in heaven and on earth under Christ" (1:10). Jesus prayed that all believers might be one (John 17:20–23), not in an organizational sense but as He and the Father are one. Twice He included the reasons for this unity: that the world might believe that Jesus came from the Father and that the Father loves the lost world. After all, if the children don't love one another, why should the world believe that the Father loves lost sinners?

The oneness of the flock is not something we must manufacture, because we are already one in Christ, whether we act like it or not. "Make every effort to keep the unity of the Spirit through the bond of peace" (Eph. 4:3). It takes effort on the part of God's people to maintain the visibility of this unity before a watching world. It isn't enough to sing, "We are not divided / All one body we"; we have to prove it by our words and actions. "So in Christ Jesus you are all children of God through faith.… There is neither Jew nor Gentile, neither slave nor free, neither male nor female, for you are all one in Christ Jesus" (Gal. 3:26, 28).

Jesus will one day gather His flock together and take them to heaven to live with Him for eternity. It will be "a radiant church, without stain or wrinkle or any other blemish, but holy and blame-less" (Eph. 5:27). Then we will be able to sing honestly, "We are not divided / All one body we." But until then, our task is to manifest God's love for the world by loving one another and loving the lost and seeking to win them to the Savior.

It isn't difficult for Christian believers to confess that Jesus is the Good Shepherd. We gladly claim Psalm 23 and rest our lives and future hopes on what it says. What is really difficult to confess is that *we are sheep and desperately need a shepherd!* We need to agree with Jeremiah's confession: "LORD, I know that people's lives are not their own; it is not for them to direct their steps" (Jer. 10:23). We also agree with Isaiah, who wrote, "We all, like sheep, have gone astray, each of us has turned to our own way; and the LORD has laid on him the iniquity of us all" (Isa. 53:6).

To claim to be one of His sheep and yet not follow Him is either to lie or to rebel, and both are terrible sins. Most of the trouble in our world is caused by people who ignore Christ and insist on having their own way, *and this can and often does happen in our local churches.* We deceive ourselves into thinking we know God's will for ourselves and everybody else, but Jeremiah 17:9 warns us, "The heart is deceitful above all things and beyond cure. Who can understand it?" When I hear a professed Christian say, "Well, if I know my own heart," I want to quote that verse from Jeremiah.

It's been my experience that the longer I follow the Lord, the more I see myself as a helpless sheep that needs Jesus the Shepherd in every decision of life. Sometimes when I forget this, He shows me a verse of Scripture to remind me, or perhaps a minor failure jolts me, or maybe a fellow believer says something that awakens me. On more than one occasion I've heard the rooster crow and my Shepherd has looked at me as He looked at Peter (Luke 22:61), and I've been humbled and broken.

When Jesus is your Shepherd and you follow Him, the future is your friend, and you don't have to be afraid.

7

THE RESURRECTION AND THE LIFE

I am the resurrection and the life. Anyone who believes in me will live, even though they die; and whoever lives by believing in me will never die.

—John 11:25–26

Do not be afraid. I am the First and the Last. I am the Living One; I was dead, and now look, I am alive for ever and ever!

—Revelation 1:17–18

Very truly I tell you, whoever hears my word and believes him who sent me has eternal life and will not be judged but has crossed over from death to life.

—John 5:24

Therefore he is able to save completely [forever] those who come to God through him, because he always lives to intercede for them.

—**Hebrews 7:25**

We were therefore buried with him through baptism into death in order that, just as Christ was raised from the dead through the glory of the Father, we too may live a new life.

—**Romans 6:4**

Praise be to the God and Father of our Lord Jesus Christ! In his great mercy he has given us new birth into a living hope through the resurrection of Jesus Christ from the dead, and into an inheritance that can never perish, spoil or fade.

—**1 Peter 1:3–4**

And this is the testimony: God has given us eternal life, and this life is in his Son. Whoever has the Son has life; whoever does not have the Son of God does not have life.

—**1 John 5:11–12**

Some of the most familiar things in life are often the most difficult to define or even to describe. For example, how would you define *light* or *cold* or describe the taste of chocolate or peppermint? How would you define *life?*

The Greek word for *life* (*zoe*) is used thirty-six times in John's gospel, which is more times than it is used in the other three gospels combined (sixteen times). We have met the word *life* in the I AM statements we have already considered, for Jesus is the bread of life (John 6:35, 48), the light of life (8:12), and the shepherd who lays down His life for the sheep (10:10, 28). In this chapter we will consider Jesus "the resurrection and the life" (11:25–26), and in the next chapter, Jesus "the way and the truth and the life" (14:6).

To the Christian believer, life is not merely a physical condition or a social experience so much as a person, and that person is Jesus Christ. Paul says that "Christ is our life" (see Col. 3:4), and he wrote to the believers at Philippi, "For to me, to live is Christ and to die is gain" (Phil. 1:21). *Life is what we are alive to!* People "come alive" to that which excites, delights, and satisfies them, that which is at the heart of their very being; and Christians should come alive to anything that relates to Jesus Christ.

Resurrection leads to life, and Jesus is both the resurrection and the life. Faith in Jesus Christ raises us from the spiritual death caused by sin (Eph. 2:1–10) and imparts to us everlasting life and abundant life. When the spirit leaves the body, the body is dead (James 2:26). For the Christian believer, this means going to be with Christ (2 Cor. 5:6–10; Phil. 1:22–23). However, if we are alive when Jesus returns, we will never die! We will be transformed as we go up to meet the Savior in the air and live with Him forever (1 Thess. 4:13–18; Phil. 3:20–21). A friend told me he hopes to go by way of the "upper-taker" and not the "undertaker," and I certainly agree with him.

The narrative in John 11 is so profound that it touches our lives in numerous ways. It deals with *love* (v. 5) and makes clear that God's love doesn't prevent God's people from experiencing pain, sickness, and sorrow. It also deals with *hope* and the loss of hope (vv. 3, 8–10, 21–22, 32). But the main emphasis is on *faith,* the faith of the disciples (vv. 1–16) and the sisters (vv. 17–44) as well as the faith of the family's friends and the Jewish religious leaders' lack of faith (vv. 45–57).

Christ is able to raise the dead and meet every need of the new life that follows that miracle, because He is both "the resurrection and the life." The Lord can move into "dead" and seemingly hopeless human situations, and by His resurrection power, transform people and circumstances and infuse life that makes everything new. Over the centuries this has happened to many local churches and other ministries as well as individual lives, *and it can still happen today!*

If you find yourself in a "dead" situation or if you are feeling a need for personal reviving (Latin, "to live again"), our Lord's statement in John 11:25–26 is the answer. Paul says that "just as Christ was raised from the dead through the glory of the Father, we too may live a new life" (Rom. 6:4). Unbelief and sin are connected with the old life of sin, but faith and life are connected with the new life in Christ. This is why Jesus commanded them to remove the grave clothes from Lazarus and give him the freshness and fragrance of new life (John 11:43–44). God's people need to get out of the grave and the grave clothes and start to manifest the new life in Christ.

As we walk through the Scriptures in our study, we will examine some instances of "resurrection and life." When you finish this chapter, I hope you will be able to give an enthusiastic "Yes!" answer to our Lord's question, "Do you believe this?" (John 11:26).

A New Nation: Israel

The nation of Israel came into being through resurrection in the lives of the patriarchs, beginning with one man and his wife—Abraham and Sarah. Israel is the most important nation God has placed on earth, because "salvation is from the Jews" (John 4:22). The Jews not only gave the world the knowledge of the one true God, but they also gave us the Bible and, most important, the Savior, Jesus Christ, the Son of God.

The Lord called Abraham and Sarah to leave their home, relatives, and idols in Ur of the Chaldees and to go to a new land He would show them. There they would begin to build a new nation that would bring blessing to the whole world. God revealed His glory to Abraham and covenanted with him to make him and his wife into a great people (Gen. 12:1–3; Acts 7:1–8). When they left Ur of the Chaldees, Abraham was seventy-five years old and his wife was sixty-five. Not only were they childless, but they were also past the age of begetting and bearing children, so how could they ever become a great nation? They felt that they were as good as dead! But that's when the miracle resurrection power of God went to work.

The fulfillment of God's promises doesn't depend on human resources but on faith in the promises of almighty God. Abraham tried to fulfill God's promise his own way by marrying his wife's

Egyptian servant, Hagar, and having a son by her, but God rejected Ishmael and gave Isaac as the heir. Faith is living without scheming, and Abraham's scheme brought trouble into his marriage as well as into his walk with God.

Abraham and Sarah both needed to experience God's resurrection power! Here's how the apostle Paul explained what had happened:

> Against all hope, Abraham in hope believed and so became the father of many nations, just as it had been said to him, "So shall your offspring be." Without weakening in his faith, he faced the fact that his body was as good as dead—since he was about a hundred years old—and that Sarah's womb was also dead. Yet he did not waver through unbelief regarding the promise of God, but was strengthened in his faith and gave glory to God, being fully persuaded that God had power to do what he had promised. (Rom. 4:18–21)

Abraham was one hundred years old when Isaac was born, and Sarah was ninety, so Isaac's birth was certainly a miracle. God was to Abraham and Sarah "the resurrection and the life." He honored their faith and gave them the resurrection power they needed to enable them to become parents. We tend to admire Abraham's faith and forget Sarah's part in this miracle. Hebrews 11:11 says, "And by faith even Sarah, who was past childbearing age, was enabled to bear children because she considered him faithful who had made the promise." Isaac was blessed with godly parents.

When Isaac was a young man, God commanded Abraham to offer him on the altar as a sacrifice, and Abraham obeyed (Gen. 22). The future of the Hebrew nation was wrapped up in that lad; but God didn't want Isaac's life, He wanted Abraham's heart. God wanted Abraham to trust Him and not the blessing God had given him. Again, it was faith in God's resurrection power that turned trial into triumph. "By faith Abraham, when God tested him, offered Isaac as a sacrifice.... Abraham reasoned that God could even raise the dead, and so in a manner of speaking he did receive Isaac back from death" (Heb. 11:17, 19). It's a wonderful thing when a father and son experience the resurrection power of the Lord.

Isaac and his wife, Rebekah, had twin sons, Jacob and Esau, and the Lord chose Jacob to inherit the covenant blessings. His story is found in Genesis 28—49. Jacob knew the Lord, but he tended to make his own plans and depend on his own clever schemes to accomplish what he wanted. He became the father of twelve sons who founded the twelve tribes of Israel.

Jacob's favorite son was Joseph. Rachel, Joseph's mother, also gave birth to Benjamin. Joseph's story is in Genesis 37—50 and tells of how ten of his brothers hated him and sold him into slavery. He ended up in Egypt and through the guidance of God eventually became second ruler of the land, but the boys lied to their father and told him that Joseph was dead. Nothing could comfort the aged patriarch, who vowed that in mourning he would go down into his own grave and join his son (Gen. 37:35). Jacob was a pessimistic man who often spoke of "going down to the grave in sorrow" (see 42:38; 44:29, 31).

But when the ten sons traveled to Egypt to get food during the seven-year famine, the Lord set in motion a process that brought Joseph and his brothers together. But even more, it brought the ten brothers to the place of repentance and confession! They returned home and told their father the truth, and Jacob experienced resurrection power and joy in his aged body and weary mind. He moved the whole family to Egypt, where Joseph had prepared places for them to live. When Jacob met Joseph in Egypt, he said, "Now I am ready to die," but he lived peacefully for seventeen more years! God graciously lifted him out of the pit of despair and gave him a new beginning. It was an emotional and spiritual resurrection.

Joseph's story begins with his seventeenth year, when God gave him two remarkable dreams and he announced them to his family (Gen. 37). The combination of his dreams and his father's preferential treatment caused his brothers to hate him. They plotted to kill him but then changed their minds and sold him as a slave. His first "resurrection" occurred when he was taken out of the pit. He became a slave to Potiphar, one of Pharaoh's officers, and eventually managed the entire household. Potiphar's wife tried to seduce him and then lied about him, and he ended up in prison. The word *dungeon* is used in Genesis 40:15 and 41:14, the same term that is used for "the pit of death" in Psalms 28:1, 30:3, 88:4, and 143:7. So, when God delivered him and made him second ruler of the land, it was like a "resurrection" from the dead. When you review the "resurrections" of Abraham and Sarah, Isaac, Jacob, and Joseph, you realize that Israel is truly a miracle nation. But there is yet another resurrection, for Paul compared Israel's future restoration to "life from the dead" (Rom. 11:15; Ezek. 37:1–14).

A New Creation: The Church

When Jesus spoke to Martha about her brother's resurrection, she affirmed her faith in that Jewish doctrine: "I know he will rise again in the resurrection at the last day" (John 11:24; see also Acts 23:8). But Jesus had quite something else in mind and replied, "I am the resurrection and the life" (John 11:25). *He moved resurrection out of a statement of faith and into a person, and out of the future and into the present.* He did not nullify the doctrine of future resurrection, but He did tell her (and us) that His resurrection power is available to His people today.

As important as doctrine is, it isn't enough for us simply to affirm what we believe. We must realize that Bible doctrine is incarnated in the Son of God and that He through the Spirit makes each doctrine real and active in our lives. "But by His doing you are in Christ Jesus, who became to us wisdom from God, and righteousness and sanctification, and redemption" (1 Cor. 1:30 NASB). Christianity is not just another religion with a statement of faith. Christianity is Christ!

Of the many pictures of salvation found in Scripture, resurrection is one of the most important and encouraging. "Very truly I tell you, whoever hears my word and believes him who sent me has eternal life and will not be judged but has crossed over from death to life" (John 5:24). Unsaved people aren't simply "sick" because of their sins; they are "dead in ... transgressions and sins.... But because of his great love for us, God, who is rich in mercy, made us alive with Christ even when we were dead in transgressions—it is by grace you have been saved. And God raised us up with Christ and seated us with him in the heavenly realms in Christ Jesus" (Eph. 2:1, 4–6). Hallelujah!

We don't know how many people Jesus raised from the dead, but three of these miracles are recorded in the Gospels. He raised a twelve-year-old girl who had just died (Luke 8:40–56), a young man who had been dead probably a day (7:11–17), and Lazarus, an older man who had been dead four days (John 11:38–44). If I were to ask you which of these persons was the most dead, you would think I had lost my mind, because *there are no degrees of death, only of physical decay.* Millions of refined, religious people live in our world who, like the little girl, give no evidence of decay, but are still spiritually dead. Others like the young man give more indication of decay, and some, like Lazarus, are quite decayed and everybody knows it. But all of them are dead!

In each instance, it was the command of His Word that restored life to these people, the same Word that today raises sinners from spiritual death when they believe in Jesus (John 5:24; Heb. 4:12; 1 Peter 1:23–25). And after they had received new life, they all gave evidence that they were indeed alive. The little girl walked about the room and ate some food; the young man spoke; and Lazarus, even though his feet were bound, came out of the cave and put on new clothes. When sinners are raised from spiritual death by the power of the living Christ, you can tell it by their walk, their talk, their appetite for spiritual food, and their rejection of the old life as they "put on" the new (Col. 3:5–17). Paul said it beautifully in 2 Corinthians 5:17—"Therefore, if anyone is in Christ, the new creation has come: The old has gone, the new is here!"

But there are two great and glorious differences between physical resurrection and spiritual resurrection. First, everybody Jesus or the apostles raised from the dead died again, but those who have been raised to eternal life can never die again. Their bodies may "sleep" in death, but their spirits will go to be with Christ forever. When Jesus returns, they will receive glorious new bodies, as will believers who are alive at His coming and are caught up in the air (1 Thess. 4:13–18).

Second, the people Jesus and the apostles raised returned to natural life, but those who have trusted Jesus since His ascension to heaven possess supernatural life in the person of the Holy Spirit. The Spirit identifies each believer with the death, burial, resurrection, ascension, and enthronement of the Savior! Read carefully Ephesians 2:4–10, Colossians 2:6–15, and Romans 6, and note Paul's prayers for God's people in Ephesians 1:15–23 and 3:14–21. Our Father wants us to live by faith in the resurrection power of Jesus Christ through the energizing ministry of the Holy Spirit.

The Holy Spirit could not be available to God's people until the Lord Jesus had died, been raised from the dead, and had ascended to heaven. "But very truly I tell you, it is for your good that I am going away. Unless I go away, the Advocate [Holy Spirit] will not come to you; but if I go, I will send him to you" (John 16:7; see also 7:37–39). The very power that raised Jesus from the dead is available to all of God's people today (Eph. 1:18–23), what Paul called "the power of his resurrection" (Phil. 3:10). This is not past history; it is present reality. Jesus says, "I am the resurrection and the life." Churches are made up of individual believers, and the Spirit must have control of those believers or nothing can be accomplished for God's glory. The "power of his resurrection" is not only saving power (Rom. 10:9–10) and keeping power (Heb. 7:25), but it is also living power (Rom. 6:4; Gal. 2:20) and serving power (Acts 1:8; 2 Cor. 5:14–15).

It's sad that so many professed Christians are like those twelve spiritually deprived men Paul met in Ephesus who did not know about the indwelling Holy Spirit (Acts 19:1–7). It's also sad that so many local churches are like the church in Laodicea that thought it had everything but was really "wretched, pitiful, poor, blind and naked" (Rev. 3:14–22). They claimed to be worshipping Jesus, yet He was outside the church door trying to get in (v. 20)!

The church doesn't depend on financial power ("Silver or gold I do not have," Acts 3:6), great intellect or talent ("They were unschooled, ordinary men," Acts 4:13), or anything the world has to offer ("My kingdom is not of this world," John 18:36). The success of the church depends wholly on the power that the Spirit gives God's people as they pray, believe, and seek to serve the Lord for His glory alone. The secret of spiritual success is not found in imitating the world's methods but in being incarnated by the Lord and His power through the ministry of the Spirit. "But you will receive power when the Holy Spirit comes on you" (Acts 1:8).

A praying and preaching church is a powerful church. The apostles gave their attention to "prayer and the ministry of the word" (Acts 6:4), for the Holy Spirit uses prayer and Scripture to accomplish His work. All prayer and no Scripture, and you end up with heat but no light; reverse it and you have all light and no heat. God wants our churches to be balanced so that the Spirit can enable us to have power for witness, work, and warfare.

A New Expectation: The Believers' Living Hope

Three New Testament epistles open with "Praise be to the God and Father of our Lord Jesus Christ." Ephesians 1:3 looks *back* and praises

God because He has blessed His people with every spiritual blessing in Jesus Christ. Second Corinthians 1:3 praises God for the *present* encouragement He gives us when things are difficult. First Peter 1:3 focuses on the *future* and praises the Father because "he has given us a new birth into a living hope through the resurrection of Jesus Christ from the dead." No Christian believer need fear death or the future because Jesus is alive and has given us a "living hope."

Peter enjoys using the word *living*. Along with the "living hope," he reminds us that the Scriptures are "living and enduring" (1 Peter 1:23) and that Jesus is the "living Stone" (2:4), while believers are "living stones" (v. 5). A "living hope" is one that does not die because it's rooted in the eternal. Aristotle defined hope as "a walking dream," and many popular hopes have turned into nightmares. Psychiatrist Karl Menninger said that hope is "an adventure, a going forward— a confident search for a rewarding life." Some hopes are froth and bubble, but when God makes a promise, you can be sure He will fulfill it. "For no matter how many promises God has made, they are 'Yes' in Christ" (2 Cor. 1:20).

As you read and ponder John 11, notice closely our Lord's words and actions. When He received the message that Lazarus was sick, He sent the messenger back with a somewhat cryptic message: "This sickness will not end in death. No, it is for God's glory so that God's Son may be glorified through it" (v. 4). The messenger faithfully delivered the message (vv. 38–40), but it didn't seem to encourage the sisters. If all Jesus was concerned about was the health of Lazarus and the sorrow of the two sisters, He could have healed Lazarus from a distance, just as He did the royal official's sick son (4:46–54) and the Roman centurion's beloved servant (Luke 7:1–10). But He wanted everyone to know that the Father gave Him permission to perform the miracle so that both the Father and the Son would be glorified and people would put their faith in Him.

Jesus sought to comfort Mary and Martha with His words, and when He came to the burial place, He wept. He knew that in a few minutes Lazarus would live again, so His tears were not for him. He wept because He beheld the pain and sorrow that sin had brought into the world, and perhaps because He knew He was calling Lazarus from a place of perfect joy to a world filled with misery. Had Mary and Martha understood and believed our Lord's message, they would have been at peace and quietly waited for Jesus to arrive at Bethany.

Jesus has promised His people, "I will come again" (John 14:3 NASB). Paul called this "the blessed hope" (Titus 2:11–14). Because Jesus is "the resurrection and the life," believers have the expectation of seeing Him, being like Him, and living with Him forever. Because Jesus is alive, this promise is a "living hope" that grows stronger and stronger in the hearts of His people. Yes, for centuries the church has been waiting and watching for His return, and there were many times when Christians forgot the promise and went to sleep. Peter tells us that this so-called delay gives the church more time to witness and unbelievers more opportunity to repent and be saved (2 Peter 3:1–10).

Believers who watch for His appearing (Matt. 25:13) will be ready when He comes, but careless Christians will be caught unprepared. Every chapter in 1 Thessalonians ends with a reference to the return of Jesus Christ and the difference this "blessed hope" should make in our lives:

- We abandon idols and serve the Lord (1:9–10).

- We love the saints and rejoice with them
  (2:17–20).

- We seek to cultivate blameless lives (3:13).

- We sorrow but not hopelessly (4:13–18).

- We major on practical holiness (5:23–24).

I recall hearing the president of a Christian university tell about a young man who was a gifted evangelist as well as a good student, and he invested his weekends preaching the gospel in churches within driving distance of the campus. He had built up a reputation that glorified the Lord, and then something happened. He began to cut back on his preaching and even his class work, and his grades began to decline. The president called him in, hoping to determine the cause of these changes, and the boy finally confessed. He had become engaged to a wonderful Christian girl and in his heart had begun to hope that Jesus would delay His return. He wanted to get married and enjoy traveling and ministering together with his sweetheart. Once that matter was settled between him and his Lord, his joy returned, his class work improved, and the power returned to his ministry.

A dear friend, now in heaven, often phoned my wife and me to chat and share prayer requests, and she ended every conversation with, "Keep looking up! It may be today!" When the "living hope" becomes a dead doctrine in the creed, our work and our witness for the Lord will gradually lose their joy and power. Please don't try to prove me wrong—it will cost you too much! The last promise in the Bible is, "I am coming soon." And the last prayer is, "Amen. Come, Lord Jesus" (Rev. 22:20).

The apostle Paul called death "the last enemy" (1 Cor. 15:26), and it is an enemy when it attacks those without faith in Christ. To the believer, death is sleep (1 Thess. 4:14; John 11:11), but keep in mind that this applies to the body and not the soul and spirit. Paul also used the word *departure* (Phil. 1:23; 2 Tim. 4:6), which in the Greek language is a rich metaphor. To the soldiers, it meant taking down the tent and moving on (2 Cor. 5:1–8), and to the sailors it means loosening the ropes and setting sail. Farmers used the word to describe removing the yokes from the oxen, and we rejoice that the dead in Christ rest from their labors (Rev. 14:13). Peter used the word *exodus* ("departure" in most English translations) to describe his approaching death (2 Peter 1:15), and Luke 9:31 uses it to describe our Lord's death on the cross. Jesus compared His own death to the planting of a seed that brings forth fruit (John 12:20–28), and Paul used the same image in 1 Corinthians 15:35–49. Psalm 23 describes the death of a Christian believer as walking safely through a valley, entering the Father's house, and living with Him forever.

In spite of the accounts we read about the near-death experiences of unsaved people seeing a bright light and losing all fear, to the unsaved person death is "the king of terrors" (Job 18:14). I recommend you read all of Job 18 and take it to heart. The resurrection of Jesus Christ declares that He is not only the Savior but also the Judge. "For he [God] has set a day when he will judge the world with justice by the man he has appointed. He has given proof of this to everyone by raising him from the dead" (Acts 17:31).

We live in a world that denies the reality of death. People don't die; they are "deceased," or perhaps have "passed away" or "left us." They are not buried but "laid to rest" or "interred." But a change in vocabulary does not alter reality: People die! Hebrews 9:27 tells us that "people are destined to die once, and after that to face judgment." But the person who trusts Jesus Christ "has eternal life and will not be judged but has crossed over from death to life" (John 5:24). Resurrection!

Christians possessed by the "living hope" will experience "hopeful living," and this hope will give them the faith and strength they need to fight the battles, carry the burdens, and keep going when life is hard. Even more, hope motivates them to encourage others and help to carry their burdens. No matter how difficult life may be, they know that Jesus has conquered the last enemy, death (Heb. 2:9–15), and that death has no dominion over them (1 Cor. 15:50–58). My friend Joe Bayly, now in heaven, wrote, "Death is the great adventure, beside which moon landings and space trips pale into insignificance."

This is because Jesus Christ is to His people "the resurrection and the life." Let's not have the "Martha mentality" and see resurrection only as a doctrine in the creed or a future event on God's calendar, for the power of Christ's resurrection is ours to experience today, as in Jesus Christ we "live a new life" (Rom. 6:4).

8

THE WAY, THE TRUTH, AND THE LIFE

I am the way and the truth and the life. No one comes to the Father except through me.

—**John 14:6**

I have chosen the way of faithfulness; I have set my heart on your laws.

—**Psalm 119:30**

There is a way that appears to be right, but in the end it leads to death.

—**Proverbs 14:12**

But when he, the Spirit of truth, comes, he will guide you into all the truth.

—**John 16:13**

The Spirit gives life; the flesh counts for nothing.
The words I have spoken to you—they are full of
the Spirit and life.

—John 6:63

Salvation is found in no one else, for there is no
other name given under heaven by which we must
be saved.

—Acts 4:12

For there is one God and one mediator between
God and human beings, Christ Jesus, himself
human, who gave himself as a ransom for all people.

—1 Timothy 2:5–6

This day ... I have set before you life and death,
blessings and curses. Now choose life, so that you
and your children may live and that you may love
the LORD your God, listen to his voice, and hold
fast to him. For the LORD is your life.

—Deuteronomy 30:19–20

The Bible records many farewell addresses. Moses gave the longest
address (thirty-three chapters in Deuteronomy), and Paul's is one of
the shortest (Acts 20:13–35). But of all the farewells given anywhere,

surely our Lord's discourse in the upper room is the deepest (John 13—16). You may read and ponder it again and again and always learn something new.

Jesus gave this discourse to prepare His disciples for His departure, because it would be their privilege and responsibility to carry on His work after He returned to heaven. First, Jesus taught them (John 13—16); next, He prayed for them (John 17); and then, He went out and died for them—and for us. At Pentecost the Holy Spirit came to empower the believers (Acts 2), and Peter's ministry that day brought three thousand people to faith in Christ.

Perhaps the most important word in the Upper Room Discourse is *Father,* which is used fifty-three times. (The word is found over one hundred times in John's gospel.) Jesus said to His Father, "I have revealed you [*your name,* Greek text] to those whom you gave me out of the world" (John 17:6), and the name He was referring to was probably "Father." In the Old Testament, you don't find God referred to as "Father" very often.[1]

Because Jesus is the way, the truth, and the life, He is able to minister to the hearts of people.

Troubled Hearts

The words *troubled* (John 14:1, 27) and *grieved* (16:6, 20–22) indicate that the atmosphere in the upper room was serious and sober. While the disciples didn't fully understand all that was transpiring that night, they knew enough to be concerned; and they were troubled for several reasons. To begin with, they were grieved because their Master was going to leave them and they didn't feel adequate for the work that lay ahead. Even more, Jesus had announced that a traitor sat at their table, and they wondered who he was. But they were all shocked when Jesus said Peter would deny Him three times! They saw Peter as their leader, and if a bold and important man like Peter failed his Lord, what might the rest of them do?

We have these same sources of sorrow in our lives today. At times we may feel our Lord has deserted us or perhaps given us work to do that is beyond our abilities. Or maybe a friend or an associate has betrayed us, or somebody we admire has fallen and failed. These experiences hurt, and they hurt us the most when we are the ones who have failed.

Our Lord assured the hearts of His disciples by speaking to them about the Father. Jesus had told them that He had come to glorify the Father (John 8:49), and that night He told them that the Holy Spirit would glorify the Son as they served Him (16:14). Children know that father and mother are there to encourage and assist them, and they call for their parents whenever trouble arises. In a similar way, our heavenly Father cares for us. When Philip asked Jesus to show them the Father, the Lord replied, "Anyone who has seen me has seen the Father" (14:9).

This helps us better understand the familiar statement in John 14:6. Jesus is the way and takes believers to the Father's *house*. Jesus is the truth and reveals the Father's *heart*. Jesus is the life and brings the Father to us so we can have His *help*. We begin the pilgrimage to the Father's house by trusting Jesus because He is the way. We continue on our journey by learning more truth about Jesus and the Father (2 Peter 3:18). We enjoy both the way and the truth because we share the life of Jesus and obey His will. "Anyone who loves me," said

Jesus, "will obey my teaching. My Father will love them, and we will come to them and make our home with them" (John 14:23). British preacher Charles Spurgeon said, "Little faith will bring your soul to heaven; great faith will bring heaven to your soul."

Jesus is the way—the *only* way—to heaven, and heaven is our final home. No matter what circumstances we may experience, knowing that we are destined for the Father's house is enough to encourage us to keep going. Whenever in our itinerant ministry my wife and I left a church or conference after the final meeting, we always experienced a quiet joy, knowing that we were going home. Our plane might be delayed, or the weather might threaten safe driving, but it made no difference because we were going home. James M. Gray, a former president of Moody Bible Institute, wrote a song with this key theme: "Who can mind the journey when the road leads home?" In the early church, the truth about life in Jesus was often called "the way" (Acts 16:17; 18:25–26; 19:9, 23; 22:4; 24:14, 22; 2 Peter 2:21).

Heaven was real to Jesus, and John emphasizes this fact in his gospel. The Father sent Jesus from heaven, a statement made thirty-eight times in John's gospel. Seven times in John 6, Jesus said that He "came down from heaven." To Him, heaven was a real place and not a state of mind, as some people want us to believe. He called heaven "my Father's house" (14:2; see also Ps. 23:6), which means it is a loving home for the family of God.

It's sad that many of God's people think of heaven only when somebody dies. Our assurance of heaven ought to be a powerful motivation each day of our lives. Abraham and the other patriarchs turned their backs on the cities of earth and focused on the heavenly city, and this helped keep them going (Heb. 11:8–10, 13–16). King David was encouraged, knowing he would meet the Lord in heaven (Ps. 17:15; 23:6), and the joy that was set before Jesus helped Him endure the cross (Heb. 12:1–2; see also Jude 24). The allurement of temptation and the burdens of pain and sorrow are diminished and often removed when we let the expectation of heaven take over in our minds and hearts, knowing that Jesus is the way.

If we choose the wrong way, we will not get closer to the Father, and this means losing the blessings He wants to give us. "Blessed are those who do not walk in step with the wicked or stand in the way that sinners take or sit in the company of mockers, but who delight in the law of the LORD and meditate on his law day and night" (Ps. 1:1–2). *If we want the full blessing of God, we must not separate the way from the Word.* To "walk in step with the wicked" means defeat, but "to keep in step with the Spirit" means victory and blessing.

Jesus is the truth, and His Word is truth (John 17:17), and we can find Him in the pages of Scripture and receive comfort and strength for the journey. The maturing believer spends time daily reading the Word and meditating on its truths, and in this way draws near to the Father's heart and is strengthened. I can recall many times in my own ministry when I felt like somebody had painted a target on my back and people were shooting at me; but then I opened my Bible and asked the Spirit to give me the truth I needed, and He never failed to meet the need. Mary A. Lathbury's words in the hymn "Break Thou the Bread of Life" describe my experience exactly: "Beyond the sacred page I seek Thee, Lord / My spirit pants for Thee, O living Word."

When you read Paul's letters and sermons in Acts, you find him frequently alluding to Scripture and quoting Scripture, because he was a man saturated with the Word of God. I believe this was one of the secrets of his endurance in those many times of stress and danger he experienced. To the believers in Rome he wrote, "For everything that was written in the past was written to teach us, so that through the endurance taught in the Scriptures and the encouragement they provide we might have hope" (Rom. 15:4). The Word believed and received provides teaching that brings encouragement, endurance, and hope.

The writer of Psalm 119 knew the blessing of getting encouragement from the Scriptures: "My soul faints with longing for your salvation, but I have put my hope in your word. My eyes fail, looking for your promise; I say, 'When will you comfort me?' Though I am like a wineskin in the smoke, I do not forget your decrees" (vv. 81–83). How do you feel when you are a "wineskin in the smoke"? Old wineskins were hung in the rafters of spare rooms, and the fire and smoke made them cracked, dry, and dirty. The people ignored them and probably wouldn't use them again. So, the psalmist felt neglected, useless, ugly, and cheap. Who cares? Who wants me? I'm worthless!

It was a wonderful day in my life when I learned that I could meet Jesus in the Old Testament as well as in the New. As I traced the cross-references from the New Testament books to the Old Testament, and vice versa, I met my Savior on page after page, and what a blessing that was! He fellowshipped with Abraham and gave him counsel (Gen. 18). He met Joshua before the battle of Jericho (Josh. 5:13–15). He shows His love for us as we read about the love of Boaz for Ruth, and He shows His care for us by His presence in the furnace with the three friends of Daniel (Dan. 3). Isaiah saw Him on His glorious throne (Isa. 6) as well as on the cross (ch. 53), and David honored Him as the exalted Son (Ps. 2) and the loving Shepherd (ch. 23).

Jesus is the way to the Father's house and the truth about the Father's heart; but He is also the one who brings us the Father's help as we abide in Him and share His life. *The will of God never leads us where the grace and power of God cannot help us and see us through.* Truth and life go together, for the truth was given to us to help us experience life and power in the Spirit. "And we also thank God continually because, when you received the word of God, which you heard from us, you accepted it not as a human word, but as it actually is, the word of God, which is indeed at work in you who believe" (1 Thess. 2:13).

How much this verse teaches us about the Bible! God's Word is a gift we have received from God, and we must accept it and thank Him for it. Christians who are not thankful for the Bible will not spend much time with the Bible. We must remember that it is *God's* Word, which means it is alive and powerful (Heb. 4:12). As we believe the Word and obey it, God's power works in us and through us and accomplishes God's purposes. God didn't give us His Word so we could explain it to others but that we might experience it ourselves and live it out for others to see the Lord. The Word must become flesh in our own lives (John 1:14) as we receive the Word and serve the Lord. "Do not merely listen to the word, and so deceive yourselves. Do what it says" (James 1:22).

Christianity is not a creed, an organization, or a religious system. It is the life of God in humans, making us more like Jesus Christ.

"God has given us eternal life, and this life is in his Son. Whoever has the Son has life; whoever does not have the Son of God does not have life" (1 John 5:11–12). The key truth is *incarnation*—"Christ lives in me" (Gal. 2:20). God's Son, God's Word, God's grace, and God's Spirit don't simply encourage us; *they enable us!* "But by the grace of God I am what I am," wrote Paul, "and his grace to me was not without effect. No, I worked harder than all of them—yet not I, but the grace of God that was with me" (1 Cor. 15:10).

Some people call this "the deeper life," others "the higher life," "the victorious Christian life," or "the exchanged life." Whatever name you give it, it is simply the life of God at work in and through us as we follow Jesus the way, believe in Jesus the truth, and surrender to Jesus the life. It's to believe that Ephesians 3:20–21 means what it says and act upon it: "Now to him who is able to do immeasurably more than all we ask or imagine, according to his power that is at work within us, to him be glory in the church and in Christ Jesus throughout all generations, for ever and ever!"

Let's all join Paul in saying, "Amen!" So be it in our lives!

Fruitful Hearts

The apostles did their work well and churches were planted in Jerusalem, Judea, Samaria, and in the Gentile world (Acts 1—10). In spite of heresies on the inside and persecutions from the outside, God's people continued to herald the gospel and many of our forbearers were faithful, so there is still a church in the world. The enemy has not overcome and the Lord continues to build His church.

But what kind of church is it? For the most part in the Western world, it certainly isn't the dynamic fellowship described in the book of Acts. In Jerusalem, the believers were together in a united fellowship (Acts 2:44), while today we are divided and competitive. The lives the early Christians lived and the good works they performed attracted attention, and people were hearing the gospel and trusting the Savior daily. The early believers had none of our modern media or promotional techniques we boast about today, but the gospel spread and the churches grew.

We glorify God by revealing Jesus in our walks, words, and works before a watching world. But if that's what it means to be a Christian, then something has gone wrong somewhere. Most of our "Christian activity" goes on in a building (also called "a church"), but we don't always see much evidence of the Lord in the home, the marketplace, or the corridors of power. Statisticians tell us that there is little difference between the divorce rate of professed Christians and that of unbelievers outside the church. All of us are embarrassed by the immorality of religious leaders—and this includes evangelicals—and we even have "Christian scams" that rob people of their money. The early church also had to contend with some of these things, but today we wish the incidents didn't occur so often.

I hear Christians complaining about the moral and spiritual darkness in the world, but if there was more light—Christian light—there would be less darkness. Experts say that things are decaying in our society, and I believe it; but if we had more salt—Christian salt—we would have less decay. "So justice is driven back, and righteousness stands at a distance; truth has stumbled in the streets, honesty cannot enter" (Isa. 59:14). We have a horrible traffic jam that neither the police nor the courts can solve! The problem lies with us, the people of God, and "it is time for judgment to begin with God's household" (1 Peter 4:17).

What we need is revival. I know that *revival* is an ancient word that may not be politically correct these days. It's not used much among Christians, unless it means "an annual evangelistic crusade." By "revival," I mean "new life, renewed life" among the people of God. Not all that we call "blessing" is from the Lord; too often it's only the result of talented human effort and not the Spirit of God; and people receive the praise, but God doesn't get the glory. In the early church, the people were "filled with awe" (Acts 2:43), but now we settle for tired business as usual.

A true blessing from God is something that God gives, says, or does that glorifies Him and meets our needs, *and you can't always explain it!* Needed money arrives unexpectedly at just the right time. The person you desperately need to see is sitting in a booth in the restaurant where you go for a cup of coffee. The old book you've been searching for shows up on the shelf of a store you didn't plan to visit. You may call these events "minor miracles," but they can be major when it comes to honoring the Lord; I know because all of them have happened to me. Bob Cook used to remind us in our Youth for Christ ministry, "If you can explain what's going on, God didn't do it."

Let's get back to John 14:6 and our desperate need for fresh life from heaven—what my friend Pastor Jim Cymbala calls "fresh wind, fresh fire."

One of God's recipes for revival is Psalm 1:1–3. It describes the type of person that God blesses and uses, and this description parallels our Lord's words in John 14:6.

Jesus is the way.

> Blessed are those
>> who do not walk in step with the wicked
>> or stand in the way that sinners take
>> or sit in the company of mockers,

Jesus is the truth.

> but who delight in the law of the LORD
>> and meditate on his law day and night.

Jesus is the life.

> They are like a tree planted by streams of water,
>> which yields its fruit in season
>> and whose leaf does not wither—
>> whatever they do prospers.

In order to receive God's blessing, we must be obedient people, the kind of people He *can* bless. "For the LORD God is a sun and shield; the LORD bestows favor and honor; no good thing does he withhold from those whose walk is blameless" (Ps. 84:11). We must be separated from the world—what John described as "the cravings of sinful people, the lust of their eyes and their boasting about what they have and do" (1 John 2:16)—and instead walk with the Lord and the Lord's people. But if the wicked, the sinners, and the people who mock the things of God are influencing our hearts and minds, then we are forfeiting the blessing of God. If we are walking in the shadows or the darkness and not in the light, and lying about it, the Lord cannot bless (vv. 5–10). God doesn't listen to our prayers if we harbor sin in our hearts *and do nothing about it.* "If I had cherished sin in my heart, the Lord would not have listened" (Ps. 66:18).

A pastor friend phoned one day and said, "Pray for us next Sunday afternoon. The church is calling a solemn assembly of confession and prayer. There's something wrong here, and only the Lord can find it and cleanse it." Along with hundreds of other people, we did pray for him and the church, and we heard later that God sent the blessing they were seeking.

I once heard a preacher say, "Years ago, we used to hear sermons about being separated from the world, but we don't preach like that today. We've matured a lot and don't need that kind of stuff today." I wanted to say to him after the service, "What you called 'that kind of stuff' is what helped to make the church what it was, a church that produced saints and soul winners." God's Word still says, "Do not be yoked together with unbelievers. For what do righteousness and wickedness have in common? Or what fellowship can light have with darkness?" (Read 2 Cor. 6:14–18.) Whether people like it or not, the Bible clearly warns us about the dangers of compromise with the world. "You adulterous people, don't you know that friendship with the world means enmity against God? Anyone who chooses to be a friend of the world becomes an enemy of God" (James 4:4). Being friendly with the world leads to "being polluted by the world" (1:27), and before long we start to "love the world" (1 John 2:15–17). This drifting eventually makes us "conform to the pattern of this world" (Rom. 12:1–2). If we don't repent and seek God's forgiveness, we will be "disciplined so that we will not be finally condemned with the world" (1 Cor. 11:32).

If you need confirmation of this sequence, review the life of Lot. As the nephew of Abraham, Lot had a wonderful opportunity to learn about the Lord and share in the covenant blessings, but he chose to pitch his tents near Sodom (Gen. 13:10–13), and then he moved into Sodom (14:1–16). Abraham rescued him once, but Lot went right back to Sodom (19:1). When the Lord was going to destroy Sodom, he sent two angels to rescue Lot and his family, but they had to take him, his wife, and two daughters by the hand and pull them to safety (ch. 19). *Lot lost everything when God destroyed Sodom!* Paul called this being saved "yet so as through fire" (1 Cor. 3:15 NKJV).

One philosophy today insists that the church must become more like the world in order to attract the world to the church, but this belief does not come from Scripture. To begin with, the early believers had no church buildings to attract people to, because the command was to go out where the people were and witness to them about Jesus. *But the less we are like the world, the more we will attract the world!* When you are different, you attract people; when you are odd, you repel them; when you are a cheap imitation, you invite their scorn. When unsaved people come into contact with Christians, *they expect them to be different.* When unsaved people visit a church, they expect the service to focus on God and not feel like they are in a religious nightclub.

This leads us to another essential for God's blessing: delighting constantly in the Word of God, for Jesus is the truth. The people God blesses don't simply read the Bible; they meditate on it and enjoy it. God's Word is seed (Luke 9:11), and when it is planted in the heart and cultivated—that's where meditation comes in—it takes root, grows, and bears fruit. Christian believers who ignore the Word or give it minimal attention are unable to bear fruit and therefore are not much of a blessing to others.

A saint who was totally yielded to God's Word wrote Psalm 119, and almost every verse in the psalm mentions the Word of God. I once read slowly through Psalm 119 and made a list of the images the writer used to tell us how much God's truth meant to him. I discovered that he would rather have God's Word than food (v. 103),[2] wealth (vv. 14, 72, 127, 162), sleep (vv. 55, 62, 147–148, 164), or even friends (vv. 51, 95, 115)! Please look up these verses, think about them, and ask yourself, "Do I love the Word of God that much?"

What we delight in is what we will sacrifice to enjoy. If we delight in the Word of God, we will gladly sacrifice sleep to be awake each morning, as did David (Ps. 57:8; 108:2) and Jesus (Isa. 50:4; Mark 1:35). We will gladly invest money in tools for Bible study, and if our witness and obedience to God's truth costs us some friends, we pray for them and trust God to give us new friends (Ps. 119:63, 74, 79). The way we treat the Bible is the way we treat Jesus, for He is the living Word and the theme of the written Word.

Jesus is the life, and abiding in Him gives us the grace and power we need for serving and obeying. The image here is that of a fruitful tree, a meaningful picture of the faithful follower of Jesus Christ. In today's world, the ideal image of many believers might be that of a tumbleweed, "blown here and there by every wind of teaching and by the cunning and craftiness of people in their deceitful scheming" (Eph. 4:14).

A healthy tree is rooted, stable, beautiful, fruitful, and useful. The roots reach to the streams of water provided by the Lord, and the believer is "rooted and grounded in love" (Eph. 3:17 NASB) as well as "rooted and built up in him [Christ]" (Col. 2:7), absorbing the water of the Holy Spirit (John 7:37–38). The vital root system brings nourishment to the trunk and branches and holds the tree steady as it grows upward. The leaves transform the sunlight into living plant tissue, and in due season, fruit appears.

The most important part of the tree is the root system, the part that nobody sees; and the most important part of the believer's life is the "root system," the part only God sees. "But when you pray, go into your room, close the door and pray to your Father, who is unseen. Then your Father, who sees what is done in secret, will reward you" (Matt. 6:6). I don't envy any child of God who is too busy to take time to be holy, whether it's in a morning watch or an evening vigil.

The tree doesn't serve itself but lives for others, and that's the attitude each Christian should have toward life. Trees don't eat their own fruit but offer it to us. (I will elaborate on the message of fruitfulness later in this book.) Trees stand in the sun and freely provide refreshing shade for the traveler. In the autumn, their leaves help to nourish the soil, and all year long their roots help to hold down the soil. The tree is healthy, and its leaves don't wither and die when they should be flourishing. During my years of pastoral ministry, I have had the sad experience of watching some of God's "trees" slowly wither, in spite of everything the congregation and I did to try to bring back spiritual health. Then the storms came and over they went.

The phrase "whatever they do prospers" refers to the blessings God sends to those whose lives He can bless. It parallels Deuteronomy 29:9: "Carefully follow the terms of this covenant, so that you may prosper in everything you do." Godly Joseph prospered (Gen. 39:2), and so did Joshua (Josh. 1:8) and Daniel (Dan. 6:28). Isaiah used a similar image: "The LORD will guide you always; he will satisfy your needs in a sun-scorched land and will strengthen your frame. You will be like a well-watered garden, like a spring whose waters never fail" (Isa. 58:11). I have noticed in my long life that some Christians can take a dying ministry and turn the desert into a garden, while some other believers will turn a garden into a desert—and the difference isn't necessarily because of talent or education. The difference is the blessing of God on a life that can be blessed.

Rebellious Hearts

John wrote his gospel to declare and defend the fact that Jesus Christ is the Son of God, the only Savior of the world and to invite his readers to put their faith in Him (John 20:30–31). As you read the gospel of John, you witness the increasing unbelief and hostility of the Jewish leaders and the growing faith and love of the disciples. Three crises appear in the book, and they are reflected in John 14:6.

The first crisis is recorded in John 6:60–66, after the feeding of the five thousand: "From that time many of His disciples went back and walked with Him no more" (v. 66 NKJV). *Jesus is the way but they would not walk with Him!* They said they walked with Abraham and even boasted that Abraham was their father (John 8:39). They claimed to be followers of Moses but rejected the one Moses wrote about (5:45–46; 9:28–29). Their unbelieving hearts were filled with rebellion against the Lord.

At the pool of Bethesda in Jerusalem, Jesus healed a man who had been sick for thirty-eight years, and He did it on the Sabbath Day (John 5). The Jewish leaders began to persecute Jesus and argue with Him because He had broken their Sabbath traditions. They were so chained to human tradition that they were blind to God's truth. They were like some people we witness to today who can speak only of their church, denomination, or religious ancestors but who know nothing about God's Word.

One day the scribes and Pharisees criticized Jesus and His disciples for not practicing the ceremonial washings before they ate, and Jesus answered them by quoting Isaiah 29:13: "These people honor me with their lips, but their hearts are far from me. They worship me in vain; their teachings are merely human rules" (Mark 7:6–7). Tradition should have a place in our lives, but human tradition must never take the place of God's truth. These skirmishes between Jesus and the religious leaders grew more and more severe until they began to plot to do away with Him (John 7:1).

The second crisis is recorded in John 12:37–38: "Even after Jesus had performed so many signs in their presence, they still would not believe in him. This was to fulfill the word of Isaiah the prophet: 'Lord, who has believed our message and to whom has the arm of the Lord been revealed?'" In His messages and miracles ("the arm of the Lord"), Jesus demonstrated who He was and what He had to offer them, yet they would not believe. Note the frightening sequence: "They … would not believe" (vv. 37–38), "they could not believe" (v. 39), which resulted in "they should not believe" (see v. 46).

Persistent hardening of the heart results in blinding the eyes and paralyzing the will. Jesus warned them, "You are going to have the light just a little while longer. Walk while you have the light, before darkness overtakes you" (v. 35), but they refused to listen. Jesus is the truth and preached the truth, *but they would not believe Him!*

The third and final crisis is recorded in John 18—19. Though Jesus is the life, *they crucified Him!* "Here is your king," Pilate said to the Jewish mob. But they shouted, "Take him away! Take him away! Crucify him! ... We have no king but Caesar!" (John 19:14–16).

There are three "rejections" in the history of Israel that we must consider: (1) When Israel asked Samuel to give them a king, they rejected God the Father (1 Sam. 8); (2) when they crucified Jesus, they rejected God the Son; and (3) when they stoned Stephen, they rejected God the Holy Spirit (Acts 7:51–60). These three rejections exhausted the longsuffering of the entire godhead. On the cross, Jesus prayed for Israel's forgiveness (Luke 23:34), and God gave the nation nearly forty years of respite; but then judgment came and Jerusalem was destroyed.

Hosea tells us the consequences: "For the Israelites will live many days without king or prince, without sacrifice or sacred stones, without ephod or household gods" (3:4). In other words, because there is no king in Israel, the nations are in tumult; and no such king will live until Jesus returns to reign. *We are living today in the book of Judges!* "In those days Israel had no king; everyone did what was right in his own eyes" (Judg. 17:6 NASB; see also 18:1; 19:1; 21:25). During the days of the judges, God raised up effective leaders here and there and gave them victories, but Israel was not united in serving the Lord and obeying His will.

When Israel's Messiah returns and they see Him and trust Him, they will mourn and repent, and a fountain will be opened to cleanse them of their sins (Zech. 13:1). "The LORD will be king over all the earth" (14:9 NASB). The more the leaders of the nations oppose one another and reject Christ, the less peace there will be in this world. When the Prince of Peace sits on the throne, there will be peace on earth.

"Pray for the peace of Jerusalem" (Ps. 122:6).

Repentant Hearts[3]

Our Lord's parable of the Prodigal Son (Luke 15:11–32) describes the spiritual condition of all who have turned their backs on God and are wasting their lives pleasing themselves. Luke 15:24 tells us the boy was lost and dead, and verse 17 reveals he was ignorant, for he had to "come to his senses." It was this ignorance of himself and what real life was all about that made him do such foolish things.

As he sat with the pigs and took inventory, he realized that his Father's house was the best place to live after all and that his father was a kind and generous man. "So he got up and went to his father" (Luke 15:20).

Jesus said, "No one comes to the Father except through me" (John 14:6). Every spiritual deficiency sinners have is met and overcome when they come to the Father through faith in Jesus Christ.

Sinners are lost, but Jesus is the way to the Father's house.

Sinners are ignorant, but Jesus is the truth about the Father.

Sinners are spiritually dead, but Jesus is the life and shares it with those who repent and trust Him.

The boy knew his life was in a mess and that it was all his fault, but that wasn't what motivated him to return home. "How many of my father's hired servants have food to spare, and here I am starving to death!" (Luke 15:17). It was not the badness of the sinner but the goodness of the father that drew him back home. Paul had that in mind when he wrote, "God's kindness is intended to lead you to repentance" (Rom. 2:4).

When he got close to home, his father saw him, ran to him, embraced him, and led him back home. The stains and smells of the far country were washed off the boy and he was given a rich garment, shoes, and a ring to wear. The past was forgiven and forgotten, and he made a new beginning.

And so may sinners today.

9

THE TRUE VINE

I am the true vine, and my Father is the gardener. He cuts off every branch in me that bears no fruit, while every branch that does bear fruit he prunes so that it will be even more fruitful. You are already clean because of the word I have spoken to you. Remain in me, as I also remain in you. No branch can bear fruit by itself; it must remain in the vine. Neither can you bear fruit unless you remain in me. I am the vine; you are the branches. If you remain in me and I in you, you will bear much fruit; apart from me you can do nothing. If you do not remain in me, you are like a branch that is thrown away and withers; such branches are picked up, thrown into the fire and burned. If you remain in me and my words remain in you, ask whatever you wish, and it will be done for you. This is to my Father's glory, that

you bear much fruit, showing yourselves to be
my disciples.

—John 15:1–8

You transplanted a vine from Egypt; you drove out
the nations and planted it. You cleared the ground
for it, and it took root and filled the land. The
mountains were covered with its shade, the mighty
cedars with its branches. Its branches reached as far
as the Sea, its shoots as far as the River. Why have
you broken down its walls so that all who pass by
pick its grapes? Boars from the forest ravage it and
wild animals feed on it.... Your vine is cut down,
it is burned with fire; at your rebuke your people
perish.

—Psalm 80:8–13, 16

I will sing for the one I love a song about his
vineyard: My loved one had a vineyard on a fertile
hillside. He dug it up and cleared it of stones and
planted it with the choicest vines. He built a watch-
tower in it and cut out a winepress as well. Then he
looked for a crop of good grapes, but it yielded only
bad fruit.... The vineyard of the LORD Almighty is
the house of Israel, and the people of Judah are the
vines he delighted in. And he looked for justice, but

saw bloodshed; for righteousness, but heard cries of
distress.

—Isaiah 5:1–2, 7

John 15:1–8 is the seventh and last of the I AM statements recorded
in the gospel of John. The first four were spoken publicly to the
crowds, the fifth privately to Martha, and the last two privately to
His disciples in His Upper Room Discourse. Using the metaphor of
the vine, Jesus explained how they could serve Him in His absence
and bear fruit for His glory. Just as a deep-sea diver survives under-
water by breathing oxygen sent down from above, so God's people
grow and serve on earth because they have a living connection with
Jesus Christ in heaven and abide in Him.

Jesus made it clear that apart from Him, they could do nothing
(John 15:5). Please note that He did not say they would be handi-
capped or disadvantaged, but that they were helpless, unable to serve
Him effectively at all. What might look like spiritual service would
be only "wood, hay or straw" (1 Cor. 3:12) and would burn up at
the judgment seat of Christ. "For from him and through him and to
him are all things. To him be the glory forever! Amen" (Rom. 11:36).
If our work doesn't begin with Christ, continue to be sustained by
Christ, and end at Christ for His glory, it will not last.

In New Testament days, the Jews were basically an agricultural
people and familiar with cultivating vineyards and making wine.
Because water was a precious commodity in the ancient Near East,
wine was a necessity and not a luxury. The prophets often used the
concept of overflowing wine vats as a description of God's blessing
(Joel 3:18; Amos 9:13; Eccl. 9:7) and a scarcity of wine as evidence of

God's discipline (Deut. 28:39, 51; Joel 1:10). The prophets also used the winepress as a symbol of judgment (Lam. 1:15; Joel 3:11–13).

In Scripture, a vine can symbolize not only Jesus Christ, but also the nation of Israel (Ps. 80:9–16; Isa. 5; 27; Jer. 2:21; 12:10–11; Ezek. 15; 17; 19:10–14; Hos. 10:1–2) and the apostate Gentile civilization on earth before Jesus returns—"the vine of the earth" (Rev. 14:14–20 NASB). In the book of Revelation, the followers of Antichrist are called "those who live on the earth" or "the inhabitants of the earth" (see Rev. 3:10; 6:10; 8:13; 11:10, 18; 13:12, 14; 14:6). Christians are citizens of heaven even though they live and serve on earth (Phil. 3:18–21), and their affection and attention are directed heavenward (Col. 3:1–4).

Just as Jesus is "the true bread" (John 6:32), so He is "the true vine," which means He is the original of which all other bread and wine are only copies. This I AM statement in John 15 has a wealth of spiritual truth in it, but I want to focus primarily on the practical truths that can help us become fruitful Christians and joyful servants.

True Living Comes from Fruit Bearing for Christ

According to Ezekiel 15, the branches of a vine are good for only two things: fruit or fuel, bearing or burning. You can't manufacture fruit, because fruit comes from life, and fruit has in it the seeds for more fruit. As branches in the vine, we can draw upon Christ's life and bear fruit for His glory. If we are not bearing fruit, we are not fulfilling our purpose on earth, and this means we are not really living. We are wasting our lives or just spending them, instead of investing them in things eternal. Believers have eternal life because they have trusted Jesus, but they may lack the "life to the full" that He came to give us (see John 10:10). They are spiritually alive but not healthy. *Fruit bearing is the "rent" we pay for the privilege of living and serving God on this earth.* It's not only our obligation as disciples of Jesus Christ, but it's also our opportunity as His servants to glorify Him and reach others.

As with the tree in Psalm 1:3, the branches of the vine don't produce fruit to feed themselves but to feed others; and it is in the feeding of others that we find our joy. Jesus said, "My food ... is to do the will of him who sent me and to finish his work" (John 4:34). Doing the will of God is not punishment; it is fulfillment and nourishment.

What is this "fruit" that Jesus expects us to bear so that we glorify Him and experience fulfilled lives? For one thing, it represents people we help lead to Christ and to maturity in the faith (Rom. 1:13). Growing in personal holiness is another fruit we harvest (6:22). In Galatians 5:22–24, Paul calls these "the fruit of the Spirit": love, joy, peace, patience, kindness, goodness, faithfulness, gentleness, and self-control. Joyful and generous giving is fruit, such as the offering Paul collected from the Gentile churches to assist the believers in Jerusalem (Rom. 15:25–28). Colossians 1:10 mentions "bearing fruit in every good work" (see also Matt. 5:13–16), and Hebrews 13:15 informs us that praise and worship are the fruit of our lips that result from the seed of the Word we have planted in our hearts.

Since fruit has in it the seeds for more fruit, Jesus spoke of our bearing "fruit, more fruit, and much fruit" (see John 15:2, 5). The harvest God gives us depends on the spiritual gifts He has given us and our faithfulness in developing them and using them as the Lord opens service opportunities for us. If we are faithful in using the few gifts and opportunities we have, the Master will reward us with many more things (Matt. 25:21). This proved true with every servant in Scripture, especially Joseph, Moses, Joshua, David, Daniel, and Timothy.

Fruit Bearing Is the Result of Abiding in Christ

Communion with Christ begins with union with Christ. We cannot have communion unless we have trusted Him, and He is our Savior, and we are in Him (2 Cor. 5:17). As branches in the vine, all believers have a living union with their Lord, and as they cultivate communion with Him, He enables them to bear fruit. It's unfortunate that the word *results* entered the Christian vocabulary ("Were there any results in the meeting last night?"), because dead machines can produce results, and so can spiritually dead religious people. Fruit is alive, and it comes out of our living communion with Jesus as His power works in and through us.

But fruit bearing requires disciplined commitment in time and effort, as well as good soil, sun and rain, and expert cultivation. We are rooted in Christ (Col. 2:7) and in love (Eph. 3:17), so the "soil" is perfect. The Father is the gardener, and He and the Son work together to enable us to bear fruit, just as the Son and the Father worked together when our Lord was ministering on earth (John 5:19, 36). Fruitless branches prove they have no living connection with the vine and they must be cut off, and fruitful branches must be pruned so they produce more and better fruit (15:1–2). Please note that when the vinedressers prune the fruitful branches, they cut away *living* wood, not dead wood, so the branch will produce better grapes. The vinedresser must know what wood to cut, how much to cut, and at what angle. It takes about three years for a professional pruner to be trained and approved.

As you read Scripture, note how the Father had to prune away good things from some of His servants so their ministries would be more fruitful and glorify the Lord in a greater way. Abraham had to leave his city and family and even offer his son Isaac to the Lord so that he might be fruitful. Jacob frequently had to lay aside his own plans so he could build the family that would give us the nation of Israel. You see this same loving process in the lives of Joseph, David, and Peter as well as in the lives of the men and women in church history who accomplished much for God's glory.

The Greek word *meno* is used eleven times in John 15, and the NIV translates it as "remain." Other English versions use "continue," "dwell," "remain in union," and "abide." "Abide" is my first choice. The Arndt and Gingrich *Greek-English Lexicon of the New Testament* says that *meno* means "an inward enduring personal communion," and that to me is "abiding." Our *union* with Christ depends totally on Him, because He always lives to intercede for us (Heb. 7:25); but our *communion* with Him depends on our faithful relationship to Him as we trust and obey.

Marriage is a good illustration of what is meant by "abiding." When the marriage ceremony ends, the official papers have been signed, and the couple has consummated the marriage, a living union has been formed and they are one flesh (Gen. 2:23–24). But union doesn't guarantee communion. Communion is something the couple has to develop and maintain between themselves. If the new husband and wife don't pray together; talk to each other; share their feelings, hopes, and disappointments; love each other; and sacrificially serve each other; their married life will become a routine or a war, and slowly lose its joy. Union is the foundation; communion is building on the foundation, and this demands mutual affection, attention, sacrifice, and service.

The fact that I am in union with Jesus Christ and a member of His body should motivate me to want to fellowship with Him and enjoy communion through worship, prayer, meditation on the Word, and service to others. "I no longer call you servants, because servants do not know their master's business," Jesus told His disciples. "Instead, I have called you friends, for everything that I learned from my Father I have made known to you" (John 15:15). The word translated "friends" means "friends at court, friends of the king." What a privileged position!

Do we meet the Lord daily and commune with Him? During the day, do we thank Him for His help and blessing? Do we trust Him to assist us in our work? Do we confess our sins immediately and keep the relationship healthy? Do we involve Jesus in the decisions we make and in the relationships and tasks that confront us? This is what it means to have communion with Christ, to abide in Him.

What are some of the evidences that we are abiding in Christ? The fact that we are bearing fruit is one of them. Although we don't always know the extent of the harvest, we see that our fruit lasts. The Scottish preacher George Morrison wrote, "The Lord rarely allows His servants to see all the good they are doing." Another evidence is that the Father prunes us and cuts away good things that are hindering us from enjoying the better and the best.

Because we are only branches, we repeatedly feel our weakness and look to the Lord for strength and help. John 15:7 promises that we will have our prayers answered. As we abide in Christ, we experience God's love (vv. 9, 12–13) and joy (v. 11), as well as the hatred and opposition of the world (vv. 18–19). We may not detect it, but as we abide in Christ, others will see us becoming more like the Lord Jesus Christ.

The evidence of true salvation in Christ and communion with Christ is fruit bearing. Judas was called by Christ, lived with Him as He ministered from place to place, and masqueraded as a converted man, but Judas was not attached by faith to Jesus the vine (John 6:60–71). Consequently, he was cut off and thrown away. "They went out from us, but they did not really belong to us. For if they had belonged to us, they would have remained with us; but their going showed that none of them belonged to us" (1 John 2:19).

Neither health nor age should hinder us from abiding in Christ and bearing fruit for His glory. "Therefore we do not lose heart. Though outwardly we are wasting away, yet inwardly we are being renewed day by day" (2 Cor. 4:16). As my wife and I become older, the Lord is teaching us to set aside some ministries (pruning) and concentrate on others, and we are discovering that it's possible to experience Psalm 92:14: "They will still bear fruit in old age, they will stay fresh and green."

Abiding in Christ Is the Result of Obeying Christ

From playing baseball to flying a jet plane, every discipline in life has laws that must be obeyed if we want to succeed. I recall a bit of poetry a chemistry professor used to quote to his first-year classes:

O shed a tear for Jimmy Brown, for Jimmy is no
more.

For what he thought was H_2O was H_2SO_4.[1]

If you want to succeed as a physician or a pharmacist, you
must learn the properties of the various elements that make up
the composition of medicine and take care that you combine only
the elements that are friendly with each other. If you don't, you
may end up joining Jimmy Brown. Aspirin and arsenic both start
with the letter A, but they have different properties. A jet pilot
dare not violate the basic principles of aeronautics nor a win-
ning athlete the official training rules and his coach's orders. By
obeying the fundamental laws that science has discovered or that
governments have enacted, we have achieved a better standard of
living and a generally safe environment. When we respect these
laws, we are able to use the power and freedom that always follow
obedience.

But there are also laws that govern our moral and spiritual lives,
and if we ignore or disobey them, we will suffer and perhaps make
others suffer. Jesus said, "If you keep my commands, you will remain
[abide] in my love, just as I have kept my Father's commands and
remain in his love" (John 15:10). Jesus always did what pleased His
Father (8:29), and if we want to abide in Him, we must follow His
example. All of nature obeys the laws that God built into the universe, but when we interfere with those laws, serious consequences
can occur.

It's a basic rule of the Christian life that faith and obedience
open the doors to God's blessing. According to Romans 14:23,

"everything that does not come from faith is sin." No matter how good we may feel about doing something, unless faith in God's Word supports our decision, what we do will only cause trouble. Abraham thought he could save his life by going to Egypt, and there he almost lost his wife and his own life (Gen. 12:10–20). Moses thought that killing a man would help deliver the Jews from Egypt, but it only led to his exile in Midian for forty years (Ex. 2:11–25). Samson thought he could fight the Lord's battles by day and enjoy the pleasures of sin by night; but God thought differently, and the strong man only crippled himself and his ministry.

Disobedience to His commands interrupts our communion with Christ, and we lose the power to do His will. When that happens, we must instantly confess our sins to the Lord (1 John 1:9) and let the Lord cleanse and heal us. To attempt to live for Christ without walking with Christ in the Spirit is futile. Remember what He said: "Apart from me you can do nothing" (John 15:5). This applies not only to our service for Christ but also to the everyday tasks of life. *Nothing goes right when our hearts are wrong.* Jonah was so sure things were going fine that he went down into the ship and went sound asleep (Jonah 1), but then he began to reap the consequences of his rebellion. The false peace and false confidence that follow willful disobedience don't last long.

Obeying Christ Results from Loving Christ

The word *obey* irritates some people, perhaps because of strict childhood discipline, or maybe a stint in the armed forces, or just the natural rebellion of the human heart. Sometimes we obey because we have to, and there is nothing wrong with that. Setting aside our own plans and learning to obey is one of the essential tasks of childhood and youth. Sometimes we obey because we have a reward in sight. ("If I mow the lawn, Dad may let me have the car Saturday.") But the best way to obey is because we want to, because we are motivated by love and not fear or greed. "If you love me, keep my commands" (John 14:15). "Anyone who loves me will obey my teaching" (v. 23).

We don't earn God's love and blessing any more than children earn their parents' love and care, but loving obedience builds character and brings joy to the parents' hearts. It means following the example of our Master. "As the Father has loved me, so have I loved you," said Jesus. "Now remain [abide] in my love. If you keep my commands, you will remain in my love, just as I have kept my Father's commands and remain in his love" (John 15:9–10). In the next verse, Jesus gives us another motive for obeying: "I have told you this so that my joy may be in you and that your joy may be complete."

"But if anyone obeys his word, love for God is truly made complete in them" (1 John 2:5). When we have mature love in our hearts, it takes the weight out of our burdens and enables us to do what needs to be done, no matter how we feel or what it costs. "This is how we know that we love the children of God: by loving God and carrying out his commands. In fact, this is love for God: to keep his commands. And his commands are not burdensome" (5:2–3).

Paul tells us in Romans 13:8 that "whoever loves others has

fulfilled the law." Our cities have laws that require parents to care for their children, but I doubt that many fathers and mothers care for their children because they don't want to go to jail. Caring for a growing family is expensive and difficult, but we do it because we love our children and want the best for them. Christian love is not hearts and flowers and fuzzy feelings. It is an act of the will as we treat others the same way the Lord treats us. "The fruit of the Spirit is love" (Gal. 5:22).

Loving Christ Results from Knowing Christ Better

"Familiarity breeds contempt" is an old adage, but it is not necessarily true. The noted American preacher Phillips Brooks said that familiarity breeds contempt "only with contemptible things and contemptible people," and he was right. My wife and I have been married since 1953 and we know each other very well, but we don't esteem each other any less, because our relationship is based on love. Frequently when driving together down the highway, we've had periods of silence—and then we will both break the silence by saying the same thing at the same time. How much better acquainted can we be!

I don't remember ordering it, but some years ago I received a biography of Adolf Hitler from a book club I belonged to, and since I paid for the book, I decided to read it. I could not. I tried but I could not. The more I read, the more I disliked the subject, and I never did finish reading the book. It was truly an experience of familiarity breeding contempt. But this could never be true of Christians reading the Bible and getting to know Jesus better, because the better we know Him, the more we love Him.

The Christian life begins with our knowing and trusting Jesus. Jesus said to His Father, "Now this is eternal life: that they know you, the only true God, and Jesus Christ, whom you have sent" (John 17:3). But as we "grow in the grace and knowledge of our Lord and Savior Jesus Christ" (2 Peter 3:18), we come to love Him more and more. In the difficult days of life as well as the delightful days, we find ourselves learning more about Him, worshipping Him, thanking Him, *and obeying Him.*

All of us are acquainted with church people who know more about popular athletes and entertainers than they do about Jesus, whom they would affirm is their own Savior. But we must learn more about Him, because the better we know Him, the more we will love Him. Every doctrine in the Bible has Jesus Christ at the very heart. Every aspect of the Christian life involves Jesus, whether it's victory over sin, praying, giving, or witnessing. One reason why some believers can't witness effectively with more loving fervor is that they are not growing in their knowledge of the Son of God.

The beautiful thing about growing in our knowledge of the Lord is that the Holy Spirit takes that knowledge and uses it to make us more like Jesus. The goal of our salvation is likeness to Christ, not just knowledge of the Bible. The Father has ordained that we should "be conformed to the image of his Son" (Rom. 8:29), and the Holy Spirit uses the Word of God to accomplish this glorious miracle (2 Cor. 3:18). "Am I becoming more and more like Jesus?" is the major question we must ask ourselves as we examine our own lives before the Lord.

Stay in Unison

"Therefore what God has joined together, let no one separate" (Mark 10:9). Our Lord was speaking about marriage, but the command applies to other areas of life as well.

God has joined together abundant living and fruit bearing. We cannot be joyful, satisfied believers unless we are bearing fruit. But God has also joined fruit bearing and abiding in Christ. We cannot manufacture spiritual fruit; it must flow out of our fellowship with the Savior. But abiding in Christ must be united to obeying, for if we disobey His Word, it damages our communion with Him and makes it difficult for Him to bless us. Obeying must be joined with loving Christ; otherwise, doing God's will becomes punishment, not nourishment (John 4:34). Finally, loving must be joined to knowing, for the better we know Christ, the more we will love Him.

To put it another way, the better we know Jesus, the more we will love Him. The more we love Him, the more we will obey Him, and the more we obey Him, the more we will abide in Him. The more we abide in Him, the more fruit we will bear; and the more fruit we bear, the more we will experience life overflowing. It's somewhat of a spiritual chain reaction, and it begins with our decision to spend quality time with our Lord each day.

10

THE NEGLECTED I AM

But I am a worm, not a human being; I am scorned
by everyone, despised by the people.

—**Psalm 22:6**

He had no beauty or majesty to attract us to him,
nothing in his appearance that we should desire
him. He was despised and rejected by others, a man
of suffering, and familiar with pain.

—**Isaiah 53:2–3**

Just as there were many who were appalled at
him—his appearance was so disfigured beyond that
of any human being and his form marred beyond
human likeness.

—**Isaiah 52:14**

How then can a mortal be righteous before God?
How can one born of woman be pure? If even
the moon is not bright and the stars are not pure
in his eyes, how much less a mortal, who is but a
maggot—a human being, who is only a worm!

—Job 25:4–6

He made himself nothing by taking the very nature
of a servant, being made in human likeness. And
being found in appearance as a human being, he
humbled himself by becoming obedient to death—
even death on a cross! Therefore God exalted him
to the highest place and gave him the name that is
above every name, that at the name of Jesus every
knee should bow, in heaven and on earth and under
the earth, and every tongue acknowledge that Jesus
Christ is Lord, to the glory of God the Father.

—Philippians 2:7–11

Psalm 22 is a messianic psalm that describes Jesus in His suffering
(vv. 1–21) and His resurrection glory (vv. 22–31). It's significant
that this vivid description of crucifixion should be found in a Jewish
psalm, because the Jews did not use this form of capital punishment,
and it is unlikely David ever saw a crucifixion. Jesus quoted verse 1
(Matt. 27:46), and the light and darkness described in verse 2 con-
nect with Luke 23:44–45. The soldiers who gambled at the foot of
the cross (v. 18) are mentioned in Matthew 27:35.

Some scholars believe that after Jesus shouted the words in Psalm 22:1, He quoted the entire psalm during His last three hours on the cross, even though His voice was unheard by the spectators. If so, then it means He quoted verse 6! If you and I had been there and heard Him, what would be our responses to what He said?

Let me share my responses to this neglected I AM as I have meditated on it over the years.

Astonishment

Up to this point, the I AM statements we have considered have all carried some dignity. There is nothing dishonorable about bread or light, shepherds or sheepfolds, resurrection or life, truth or vines; but worms are quite another matter. Apart from professional entomologists, very few people find much in worms to admire. Worms are dirt dwellers that are despised and often stepped on. When you consider that Jesus is the one speaking, the statement is astonishing.

When Job described himself in his suffering, he said that corruption was his father and the worm his mother or sister (Job 17:14), and that his body was "clothed with worms" (7:5). Job's friend Bildad said humans are maggots and worms (25:6). The prophet Isaiah described the judgment of the wicked like this: "Their worm will not die, nor will their fire be quenched" (Isa. 66:24). Because he was a proud and bloodthirsty ruler, Herod Agrippa I was "eaten by worms and died," an ignominious end for a king (Acts 12:21–24).

Originally it was David who made the statement "I am a worm," but David was a prophet and wrote about Christ (Acts 2:30). Psalm 22 is about Jesus, the Son of God, and He is calling

Himself a worm! Hebrews 7:26 describes Him as "holy, blameless, pure, set apart from sinners, exalted above the heavens," yet He calls Himself a worm. Other people have expressed self-reproach, but they weren't as holy or as exalted as Jesus. Job said to the Lord, "I am unworthy—how can I reply to you? I put my hand over my mouth.… Therefore I despise myself and repent in dust and ashes" (Job 40:4; 42:6). Paul called himself the worst of sinners (1 Tim. 1:15), "the least of the apostles" (1 Cor. 15:9), and "less than the least of all the Lord's people" (Eph. 3:8). *But the Son of God called Himself a worm!*

The statement becomes even more astounding when we remember that He was speaking to His heavenly Father, whose will He had obeyed during all His years of ministry on earth. It was the Father who said of Him, "This is my Son, whom I love; with him I am well pleased" (Matt. 3:17). But even more, when we consider when He spoke these words, they become incredible. *It was while He was doing His greatest work and dying on the cross for the sins of the world!* While committing some selfish, abominable sin, anybody could say, "I am a worm," but certainly not while doing the greatest work ever done on earth and experiencing the greatest suffering.

Adoration

Contemplating the depth of our Lord's humiliation ought to move us to adoration and worship. At His incarnation He became human and was born a human and a servant; and at His crucifixion He became "a worm and not a man" (Ps. 22:6 NASB). New Testament scholars call the first year of our Lord's public ministry "the year of popularity," because great crowds of people sought Him and opposition had not yet begun. But by the third year of our Lord's ministry, the religious leaders were envious and angry and were plotting to kill Him. No employee in the American penal system today would dare to treat the worst criminal in the cell block the way Jesus was treated.

Our Lord became "a worm and not a man" socially. He was called a glutton and a drunkard (Luke 7:34) and even a demoniac (John 8:48); and another messianic psalm says, "Those who sit at the gate mock me, and I am the song of the drunkards" (Ps. 69:12). When they should have been obeying Him, the people were making fun of Him. As opposition increased and His death drew nearer, Jesus sometimes left Jerusalem and Judea and went to secluded places to pray and teach His disciples. But the officials of the nation had already classified Him with the lowest of the low, "a friend of tax collectors and sinners" (Luke 7:34).

Jesus was treated like "a worm and not a man" as far as the law was concerned. His arrest was illegal and so was His trial. The Jewish leaders paid false witnesses to testify against Him, and even though they contradicted each other, the judges accepted their testimony. They considered Jesus guilty even before the trial began.

He was treated like "a worm and not a man" as far His physical body was concerned, because they whipped and beat Him as if He were an animal. What do you do to a worm? You step on it and crush it. The brutal treatment by the soldiers was unnecessary and inhuman. But Psalm 22 uses animals to depict the soldiers and officials, not the Savior. "Many bulls surround me; strong bulls of Bashan encircle me. Roaring lions that tear their prey open their mouths wide against me" (vv. 12–13). "Dogs surround me, a pack of villains encircles me; they pierce my hands and my feet" (v. 16). "Deliver me from the sword, my precious life from the power of the dogs. Rescue me from the mouth of the lions; save me from the horns of the wild oxen" (vv. 20–21).

But the first verse of Psalm 22 gives us the most painful reason why Jesus said He was "a worm and not a man": "My God, my God, why have you forsaken me?" (See also Matt. 27:46.) Many people have forsaken God, but God has never forsaken anyone, for if He did, they would instantly die. "God … is not far from any one of us," Paul told the Greek philosophers. "For in him we live and move and have our being" (Acts 17:27–28). Cain forsook God, but God didn't forsake Cain (Gen. 4). The nation of Israel repeatedly rebelled against the Lord, but He continued to love them, discipline them, and call them to repentance. "I, the God of Israel, will not forsake them" (Isa. 41:17).

Why did the Father forsake His beloved Son? Because He was the "lamb of God" on whom the Father laid "the iniquity of us all" (Isa. 53:6; see also John 1:29). "God made him who had no sin to be sin for us, so that in him we might become the righteousness of God" (2 Cor. 5:21). When Christ became sin and the sin offering, the Father turned away from His own Son, because God's "eyes are too pure to look on evil" (Hab. 1:13). Every time we meet at the Lord's table, we are reminded that the punishment we should bear because of our sins, He bore for us. "This is my body given for you.… This cup is the new covenant in my blood, which is poured out for you" (Luke 22:19–20). For *you!* Paul wrote that "the Son of God … loved me and gave himself for me" (Gal. 2:20). For *you!* For *me!*

Shame

Scripture uses many different images to describe sin and sinners—lost sheep, lost coins, blind wanderers, rebels, corpses, hopeless prisoners, and slaves, to name just a few. But if Jesus became on the cross what we sinners really are, *then we are worms!*

Isaac Watts wrote in a hymn, "Would He devote that sacred head / For such a worm as I?" But some contemporary hymn editors have replaced the "worm" line with "for sinners such as I." We don't mind being called sinners, but we don't like being called worms. *But that's what we are!* Editors can remove the word *worm* from the hymnal but not from the Bible.

We think we are so big and powerful, when in God's sight we are only small and feeble. "Surely the nations are like a drop in a bucket; they are regarded as dust on the scales; he weighs the islands as though they were fine dust" (Isa. 40:15). Pharaoh didn't frighten the Lord when Moses told the Egyptian leader what to do, and neither did Sennacherib or Herod or Caesar. God easily defeated all of them. "But God chose the foolish things of the world to shame the wise; God chose the weak things of the world to shame the strong" (1 Cor. 1:27).

God knows us thoroughly. In the Scriptures He tells us what we are, and we had better agree with Him. But what we are in ourselves isn't important; it's what we are in Christ that really counts. God still uses the weak things to triumph over the strong and to silence those who boast. No matter how far along we are in our faith journey, it does us good to recall what we used to be and what the Lord has done for us. In Isaiah 41, the Lord is encouraging His people Israel and calls them "my servant ... whom I have chosen" (v. 8). He promises, "I will strengthen you and help you; I will uphold you with my righteous right hand" (v. 10). But right in the middle of the chapter, He calls them "you worm Jacob, little Israel" and promises to make the little worm into a threshing sledge with many sharp teeth (vv. 14–15)! Have you ever seen a worm with teeth that was able to grind mountains into sand?

We should not stare into the mirror and groan, "I'm a worm— I'm nothing." We know what we are and we also know *what we are in Christ by faith!* Whenever we are ashamed of what we are in ourselves, we should be assured by what we are and what we have in our loving Savior. There is a place in the Christian life for shame and humility: "'God opposes the proud but shows favor to the humble and oppressed.' Humble yourselves, therefore, under God's mighty hand, that he may lift you up in due time" (1 Peter 5:5–6).

Astonishment, adoration, and shame lead the way to at least one more response.

Gratitude

Most hymnals don't include the verse of Isaac Watts' hymn that I mentioned above, so here it is:

> Thus might I hide my blushing face
> While His dear cross appears,
> Dissolve my heart in thankfulness,
> And melt my eyes to tears.

Sincere tears and thankfulness are two marks of the spiritual believer; dry eyes and a hard heart usually belong to the nominal

Christian or the worldly one. One of the most difficult things to maintain in the spiritual life is a tender heart that is burdened enough to weep and pray as well as watch and pray.

Nicodemus and Joseph of Arimathea lovingly wrapped the body of Jesus in strips of linen, while sprinkling in about seventy-five pounds of spices; then they laid our Lord's body in Joseph's new tomb. But three days later, the wrappings were empty and the body of Jesus was gone! The neat wrappings looked like an empty cocoon after a beautiful butterfly had emerged. Jesus the "worm," once treated so mercilessly, was now alive and wearing a robe of glory! Hallelujah!

Psalm 22:22–31 deals with the postresurrection words and ministry of Jesus, climaxing with "They will proclaim his righteousness, declaring to a people yet unborn: He has done it!" Some students equate the phrase "He has done it" with the Lord's cry from the cross, "It is finished" (John 19:30).

Over the years, I've noticed what appears to me a decline in personal gratitude among people, as though we are entitled to what others do for us; and I fear this attitude is creeping into the church. We tend to take things for granted—until we lose them! People have many different devices today for communicating with each other, but how many times are the words *thank you* transmitted? I also wonder how much time we spend thanking the Lord for His bounteous grace and goodness. I say it again: Are we taking for granted the gifts and services we receive from God and others? I hope not.

If this neglected I AM does nothing else for us, it should improve our perspective on life and Christian service. "Who dares despise the day of small things?" the Lord asked the prophet Zechariah (Zech. 4:10). Everybody has a very small beginning in conception and as a baby, a new student in school, a beginning employee, a husband or wife. We all have times of failure and frustration when we can honestly say, "I am a worm," but we need to say it *more* in times of success and recognition. Like David, we must pray, "Who am I, Sovereign LORD, and what is my family, that you have brought me this far?" (2 Sam. 7:18).

Never be afraid to make a small beginning for the Lord. He is willing to meet with just two or three people (Matt. 18:20). Jesus began His earthly ministry as a baby in a manger. Many a great ministry has started with a small prayer meeting or a small offering. J. Hudson Taylor opened the China Inland Mission bank account with ten British pounds. The young lad gave his small lunch to Jesus, and He fed thousands. I used to remind my pastoral students, and I still remind myself, that there are no small churches and there are no big preachers, but we do serve a great and glorious God.

11

"I Am Jesus"

(Acts 9:5; 22:8; 26:15)

She will give birth to a son, and you are to give him
the name Jesus, because he will save his people from
their sins.

—Matthew 1:21

When he [Bartimaeus] heard that it was Jesus of
Nazareth, he began to shout, "Jesus, Son of David,
have mercy on me!"

—Mark 10:47

Above his head they placed the written charge
against him: this is Jesus, the king of the Jews.

—Matthew 27:37

Then he [the thief on the cross] said, "Jesus, remember me when you come into your kingdom." Jesus answered him, "Truly I tell you, today you will be with me in paradise."

—**Luke 23:42–43**

God has raised this Jesus to life, and we are all witnesses of the fact. Exalted to the right hand of God, he has received from the Father the promised Holy Spirit and has poured out what you now see and hear.... Therefore let all Israel be assured of this: God has made this Jesus, whom you crucified, both Lord and Messiah.

—**Acts 2:32–33, 36**

Salvation is found in no one else, for there is no other name given under heaven by which we must be saved.

—**Acts 4:12**

But Stephen, full of the Holy Spirit, looked up to heaven and saw the glory of God, and Jesus standing at the right hand of God.

—**Acts 7:55**

Therefore God exalted him [Jesus] to the highest place and gave him the name that is above every name, that at the name of Jesus every knee should bow, in heaven and on earth and under the earth, and every tongue acknowledge that Jesus Christ is Lord, to the glory of God the Father.

—Philippians 2:9–11

He who testifies to these things says, "Yes, I am coming soon." Amen. Come, Lord Jesus.

—Revelation 22:20

Strictly speaking, "I am Jesus" doesn't qualify as an I AM statement; but I have two excellent reasons for including it: First, it is always right to magnify Jesus; and second, the statement is found three times in the book of Acts, and repetition suggests importance. I don't want to conclude this book without again presenting Jesus our Lord and Savior, lest there be even one reader who has never trusted Him personally and experienced the new birth.

Before you read this chapter, I suggest you first read Acts 9:1–31, which is Dr. Luke's account of Paul's conversion; and then read Paul's two personal accounts in Acts 22 and 26. Paul's first account was given before an angry Jewish mob in the temple at Jerusalem, and his second as part of his legal testimony before King Agrippa II and the Roman governor Porcius Festus. The basic facts are the same in each narrative, but there are some differences that help to bring out some special truths. Keep in mind that Saul of Tarsus was converted while going on a week's journey from Jerusalem to Damascus, a distance of about 150 miles.

This chapter is built around seven stages in Paul's Damascus Road encounter that transformed him from Saul of Tarsus the rabbi into Paul the apostle of Jesus Christ to the Gentiles.

He Saw a Light (Acts 9:3; 22:6; 26:13)[1]

Luke wrote that "suddenly a light from heaven flashed around him [Paul]," and Paul told the Jews "a *bright* light from heaven flashed around me." His description to Festus and Agrippa was "I saw a light from heaven, *brighter than the sun, blazing* around me and my companions." Note the sequence: a light, a bright light, a light brighter than the sun. This reminds us of Proverbs 4:18: "The path of the righteous is like the morning sun, shining ever brighter till the full light of day."

Light was an important metaphor to Paul.[2] He took Isaiah 42:6–7 personally and made it a key verse in his life: "I, the LORD, have called you in righteousness; I will take hold of your hand. I will keep you and will make you to be a covenant for the people and a light for the Gentiles, to open eyes that are blind, to free captives from prison and to release from the dungeon those who sit in darkness." (See also Acts 13:47; 26:15–18, 23.)

Paul had always believed that the Gentiles were living in spiritual darkness, because that was a basic tenet in Hebrew theology. But now God made it clear to Paul that he, a Jew, was also in spiritual darkness! In his masterful letter to the Romans, Paul explains that God didn't ask the Gentiles to go higher and become like the Jews;

He told the Jews they were on the lowest level with the Gentiles. "There is no difference between Jew and Gentile, for all have sinned and fall short of the glory of God" (Rom. 3:22–23). What a humiliating blow!

Seeing ourselves as God sees us and admitting our great need are the first steps toward becoming a child of God. Paul could brag to himself and others about his first birth (Phil. 3:4–11; Gal. 1:11–17), but he could not boast about anything before the throne of God. "Where, then, is boasting? It is excluded" (Rom. 3:27). Changing our minds and telling the truth about ourselves and Jesus is what the Bible calls *repentance;* and like every lost person, Paul needed to repent. Before conversion, there must be conviction, and there is evidence that Paul was being convicted about his sins—but more about that later.

The rebellious rabbi was about to enter into the new creation (2 Cor. 5:17), and God said, "Let there be light" (Gen. 1:3). Years later Paul could ask, "Have I not seen Jesus our Lord?" (1 Cor. 9:1).

He Fell to the Ground (Acts 9:4; 22:7; 26:14)

When we compare Acts 9:7; 22:10; and 26:14, we learn that the men who accompanied Paul also fell to the ground but then got up again, while Paul remained facedown. "Pride goes before destruction, a haughty spirit before a fall" (Prov. 16:18), but in this case, his fall would lead to salvation, not condemnation. It would fulfill the prophecy that aged Simeon spoke to Mary: "This child [Jesus] is destined to cause the falling and rising of many in Israel" (Luke 2:34). Note the sequence: Pride leads to a fall that humiliates us, but humility leads to a fall *that elevates us and leads to our rising again to a new life!* "God is opposed to the proud, but gives grace to the humble" (1 Peter 5:5 NASB); and the grace that comes from the highest place, where God reigns, is found only in the lowest place where we surrender to the Lord.

I think it was Andrew Murray who said that humility is not thinking meanly of ourselves but simply not thinking of ourselves at all. Truly humble people do not surround themselves with mirrors reflecting only themselves. Instead, they surround themselves with windows through which they can see others and discover their needs. Jesus not only spoke to crowds but also took time to listen to individuals and meet their needs. He humbly was at the beck and call of lepers, beggars, foreigners, and even dying criminals!

Humility is the soil out of which all other Christian virtues may grow. Proud people love themselves, not others, and if they pay any attention to others, it's only to use them to promote themselves. Proud people enjoy very little peace because they are always fearful of being upstaged by somebody. Proud people have very little patience with the ordinary people around them, and as for being kind and gentle toward others, they rarely think about it. G. K. Chesterton wrote, "Pride is a poison so very poisonous that it not only poisons the virtues, it even poisons the other vices." Read that statement again and ponder it.

When D. L. Moody was directing the Northfield Schools in Massachusetts, one day he was in his carriage at the railway station, waiting for some students to arrive. Suddenly, a man ordered him to help him and his daughter with their luggage and then take them to the school. Moody jumped down and loaded the baggage on the carriage and drove to the campus. A short time later when the father entered the office to register his daughter, he was shocked to discover that the man he had been ordering around was the president of the school. Moody only chuckled and tried to put him at ease, but the father had learned a good lesson. In one of his sermons, Mr. Moody said, "If we are going to be used of God, we have to be very humble.... The moment we lift up our head and think we are something and somebody, He lays us aside."[3]

He Heard a Voice (Acts 9:4; 22:7; 26:14)

The voice said, "Saul, Saul, why do you persecute me? It is hard for you to kick against the goads" (26:14). The men with Paul heard a sound from heaven but could not distinguish the words, and Paul had no idea who was speaking! However, before the speaker identified Himself, He revealed what Saul of Tarsus really was: an angry animal that wanted his own way and was rebelling against the Lord who was prodding him with conviction. (See Acts 8:1–3; 9:1.) Paul considered himself a devout and zealous rabbi, a defender of God's holy law, so being called an angry animal was a shocking experience for him. Actually, this indictment was one more step in God's gracious process of humbling Paul.

In the ancient Near East, an ox goad was a pole about eight feet long, with a small spade at one end (for scraping off mud) and a sharp point at the other. The farmer would prod the oxen and keep at it until the animals obeyed. This raises a fascinating question: Prior to his conversion, what was Rabbi Saul experiencing in his mind and heart that finally brought him to faith in Christ? How did God

prepare this fanatical persecutor to trust Jesus when he was sure Jesus
was only a dead deceiver? (See Matt. 28:1–15.)

I think one of the strongest "goads" the Lord used was the tri-
umphant witness of Stephen, the first Christian martyr (Acts 6—7).
It's probable that Paul heard Stephen preach in the Synagogue of the
Freedmen in Jerusalem, since Jews from Cilicia were there (6:9), and
Paul was from Tarsus, the capital city of Cilicia. If Paul was in that
synagogue congregation, then he was not able "to stand up against
the wisdom the Spirit gave him [Stephen] as he spoke" (6:10); and
this must have infuriated the young rabbi. Paul heard Stephen's powerful sermon, and he saw Stephen's radiant face. When Stephen was
stoned to death, Paul not only approved of the murder but also took
care of the garments of the men who killed him (7:58; 8:1).

When he spoke to the angry Jewish mob in the temple, Paul
openly admitted that he could not forget the death of Stephen
(Acts 22). He told them what he had said to the Lord when He
appeared to him in the temple: "Lord … these people [the Jews]
know that I went from one synagogue to another to imprison
and beat those who believe in you. And when the blood of your
martyr Stephen was shed, I stood there giving my approval and
guarding the clothes of those who were killing him" (vv. 19–20).
Stephen's sermon, his vision of Jesus, his prayer of forgiveness for
his murderers, and the glory of God on his face all were goads that
certainly cut into Paul's heart. No doubt many of the believers
Paul arrested and jailed also gave a witness that was so consistent
that he could not ignore it.

Another painful goad was the frustration he must have experienced as he tried in his own strength to keep God's law as he was

"advancing in Judaism" (Gal. 1:14). Personally, I don't interpret Romans 7 as a description of Paul's preconversion experience. But if Romans 7 describes the struggle he felt *after* his conversion, what must he have experienced *before he was converted!* The more he tried in his own efforts to be a successful Pharisee, the more he uncovered deeper sins in his heart and the more frustrated he became. After all, Paul didn't have copies of Romans 6—7 or Galatians 3—5; after his "schooling" in Arabia for three years, later he would write them. But as a young rabbinical student studying the Old Testament law, he must have repeatedly discovered how weak he really was. He appeared to be a model religious leader, but in his own heart, he knew he was stumbling and failing. His face had never been as radiant in life as Stephen's was in death.

In his superb book *A Man in Christ,* Dr. James S. Stewart writes, "And here at once we meet the striking fact that for years before the call came the dominating note of Paul's inner life had been one of utter failure and frustration and defeat.... He found that the more keenly he pursued his ideal, the farther it receded. The righteousness on which his heart was set stood afar off, mocking his endeavor."[4] James Stalker wrote in *The Life of St. Paul,* "On the contrary, the more he strove to keep the law the more active became the motions of sin within him; his conscience was becoming more oppressed with the sense of guilt, and the peace of a soul at rest in God was a prize which eluded his grasp."[5]

Like many religious people today, Paul was serious and sincere, but he was unable to grasp the meaning of what it meant to receive God's righteousness by faith in Jesus Christ, the gift of God's grace. Why would anybody want to follow an unemployed Jewish carpenter

from Nazareth who was crucified by the Romans? To his educated
intellect, it all seemed foolish.

He Asked a Question (Acts 9:5; 22:8; 26:15)

A young Jewish student asked his teacher, "Rabbi, why is it that
whenever I ask you a question, you always answer with another question?" The rabbi replied, "So why shouldn't I?"

Paul knew how to ask the right questions and cried, "Who are
you, Lord?" The word translated "Lord" could be only a respectful
"sir," or it might convey reverence as to God; we aren't sure which
meaning Paul intended. But he received a profound answer: "I am
Jesus of Nazareth, whom you are persecuting." To his amazement,
Paul discovered that not only was Jesus alive (Acts 25:19), but He
was so identified with His people that whoever persecuted them also
persecuted Him. In his blind religious zeal, Paul had been persecuting his own Messiah! Paul may have been present at the meeting
of the Sanhedrin when the Jewish leaders commanded Peter and
John "not to speak or teach at all in the name of Jesus" (4:18), and
certainly he agreed with the verdict; but now things would change.

The name *Jesus* is found more than nine hundred times in the
original text of the New Testament and more than sixty times in the
book of Acts. Acts 4:12 states boldly, "Salvation is found in no one
else, for there is no other name given under heaven by which we
must be saved." Every New Testament book except 3 John mentions
the name *Jesus,* but verse 7 of 3 John reads, "It was for the sake of the
Name that they went out...." The name of Jesus opens and closes the
New Testament (Matt. 1:1; Rev. 22:21). It is the name we use when

we pray (John 14:13–14; 15:16; 16:23–26), and it is the name of Jesus that the world hates (15:18–24).

Jesus (*Yeshua*) was a popular name among the Jews because of the fame of Joshua, successor to Moses, who brought Israel victoriously into their promised land. The Jewish historian Josephus lists twenty different men with that name. The name means "Jehovah is salvation" (see Matt. 1:16, 21, 25). Since other men also had that name, our Savior was known as "Jesus the Christ" or "Jesus of Nazareth." In the second century, the Jews stopped naming their sons "Yeshua."

He Surrendered to Jesus (Acts 22:10)

By the fourth stage in Paul's crisis experience, he had been arrested, blinded, humbled, and taught. He knew what he was and what he really had been doing, and he knew that he was speaking to the Messiah, Jesus Christ. Paul was now ready to trust and obey, and he asked, "What shall I do, Lord?" The fullest reply to this question is in Acts 26:16–18:

> Now get up and stand on your feet. I [Jesus] have appeared to you to appoint you as a servant and as a witness of what you have seen and will see of me. I will rescue you from your own people and from the Gentiles. I am sending you to them to open their eyes and turn them from darkness to light, and from the power of Satan to God, so that they may receive forgiveness of sins and a place among those who are sanctified by faith in me.

Paul had begun this trip leading a group of zealous Jews to battle, and now one of those men took blind Paul by the hand as though he were a little child and led their leader to Damascus. Paul was humble now and willing to obey, and for three days he sat in the darkness and ate no food. Then the Lord sent one of the ordinary believers in the city to restore Paul's sight, impart the fullness of the Spirit to him, and baptize him. Were it not for Paul, we would never have met Ananias; but were it not for Ananias, Paul could not have entered into his ministry. He spent time with the believers in Damascus and began boldly preaching in the synagogues.

What Jesus said to Paul was simply, "Get up! Stand up! Speak up! Look up!" But isn't this what He says to all of His followers, including you and me?

He Obeyed Christ's Orders (Acts 26:19–23)

Paul said at his trial, "So then, King Agrippa, I was not disobedient to the vision from heaven." Paul, the leader of opposition against Jesus, was now being led by Jesus, and the persecutor was now a preacher. The man who had caused others to suffer would himself suffer greatly as both Jews and Gentiles opposed his ministry and his message. If you need to be reminded of some of Paul's ministry pains, or if you think your own situation is unbearably difficult, read 2 Corinthians 4:1–12 and 11:16–29.

If we were to ask Paul, "What did the Lord do to you throughout that entire experience on the Damascus road?" he might refer us to Philippians 3:12–14 and underline the words "Jesus took hold of me" (v. 12). Our King James Version uses the word "apprehended," which means "to seize, to grasp, to get your hands on." *God arrested Paul!* God put one hand on Paul and the other hand on His will for Paul and brought them together and kept them together throughout Paul's ministry. He wrote that his consuming desire was "to take hold of that for which Christ Jesus took hold of me" (v. 12), and that same desire should control us.

He Spread the Message (Acts 26:23)

He had seen the light and from now on would "bring the message of light" to both Jews and Gentiles. Paul saw himself as an ambassador of Jesus Christ, commissioned by the Lord and motivated by His love (2 Cor. 5:14, 20). Ambassadors must deliver faithfully only the messages their superiors deliver to them, and the message Jesus gave to Paul was the gospel. "I am compelled to preach," he said. "Woe to me if I do not preach the gospel!" (1 Cor. 9:16).

Every Christian minister, teacher, and musician must carefully examine each sermon, lesson, and song and ask, "Where is Jesus? Where is the gospel?" We are not ministering to display our talents or exalt ourselves but to glorify Jesus Christ. "May I never boast," Paul wrote, "except in the cross of our Lord Jesus Christ" (Gal. 6:14). Paul's goal was "that in everything he [Jesus] might have the supremacy" (Col. 1:18). The purpose of ministry is not to impress people but to express the truth of Jesus and the gospel.

We are servants, not celebrities, and when the church assembles in the name of Christ, it is for worship that honors God and not for entertainment that makes people feel good. As my wife and I walked into a church one Sunday, the greeter said, "Welcome! Come in and have fun!" I almost turned around and walked out. Did the prophet Isaiah "have fun" when he worshipped the Lord (Isa. 6) or the apostle John when he saw his glorified Savior (Rev. 1:9–18)? Both of them saw Jesus, and this gave them new spiritual vision and vitality to serve Him effectively.

He says to us today, "I am Jesus!"

"Therefore, since we are receiving a kingdom that cannot be shaken, let us be thankful, and so worship God acceptably with reverence and awe, for our 'God is a consuming fire'" (Heb. 12:28–29; see also Deut. 4:24).

12

LIVING AND SERVING IN
THE PRESENT TENSE

I tell you, now is the time of God's favor, now is the
day of salvation.

—**2 Corinthians 6:2**

History is so often being rewritten these days that we may not know exactly what has happened in the past; and since we are not omniscient, we cannot predict the future accurately. However, there is still good news: Right now, in this present hour, God gives us the privilege of making decisions that may alter some of the consequences of the past and also help establish some exciting new directions for the future. "I tell you, now is the time of God's favor, now is the day of salvation" (2 Cor. 6:2). Now! Today!

God wants His children to live a day at a time, in the present tense, trusting in His guidance and grace. "Give us this day" applies not only to our daily bread but also to everything else involved in our day-by-day pilgrim journey. From the first day of creation, the Lord ordained that our galaxy function a day at a time as Planet Earth makes its annual trip around the sun. The next time you say, "I wish I had more time," remind yourself that we all have the same amount of time—twenty-four hours a day—and that perhaps we should be saying, "I wish I had more control over my time." This means being wise and "making the most of every opportunity, because the days are evil" (Eph. 5:15–16).

On April 24, 1859, the American naturalist Henry David Thoreau wrote in his journal, "Now or never! You must live in the present, launch yourself on every wave, find your eternity in each moment." In the first chapter of *Walden,* Thoreau wrote, "As if you could kill time without injuring eternity," a remarkable statement from a man who "signed off" from the church early in his life. But he is right: If we thought more about eternity, we would certainly use our time more wisely.

Time is one of our most precious treasures, a moment-by-moment gift from God, and it's a shame to spend it carelessly or waste it foolishly. With the Lord's help, we can transform time into service, learning, wealth, pleasure, health, and spiritual growth. Even though we appreciate what Jesus did for us yesterday and eagerly anticipate what He will do in the future, the key words for the church are *now* and *today.* After all, our Savior "is the same yesterday and today and forever" (Heb. 13:8), and as we have learned from His I AM statements, He is the Jesus of the present tense.

The four gospels report what Jesus "began to do and to teach" in His physical body while on earth (Acts 1:1), but the word *began* indicates that He wants to continue to "do and to teach" today through His spiritual body, the church. The coming of the Holy Spirit at Pentecost (ch. 2) was a beginning, not an ending, and the Spirit wants to work through us today. Quoting from Psalm 95, the Holy Spirit says in Hebrews 3:7–11:

> Today, if you hear his voice, do not harden your hearts as you did in the rebellion, during the time of testing in the wilderness, where your ancestors tested and tried me, though for forty years they saw what I did. That is why I was angry with that generation; I said, "Their hearts are always going astray, and they have not known my ways." So I declared on oath in my anger, "They shall never enter my rest."

"The rebellion" refers to Israel's disobedience that began at Kadesh Barnea when they refused to trust the Lord and claim their inheritance in Canaan (Num. 13—14). That rebellion continued for the next thirty-eight years as the nation wandered in the wilderness until the unbelieving older generation died off. The disobedience of ten leaders corrupted the nation and eventually led to a long funeral march.

My wife and I have had our share of tests and trials during our years of ministry, times when we alone or we and our people were tempted to give up instead of trusting God to keep things going. We praise God for giving us His promises from the Word and also for surrounding us with praying people who walked by faith and whose prayers, joined with ours, helped to see us through.

When Israel in unbelief rebelled against God, part of the problem was the people's focus on the past and their repeated desire to go back to Egypt. They remembered the food they ate and the security they enjoyed because somebody took care of them, but they had forgotten the daily bondage, humiliation, and hopelessness. Another cause of their unbelief was fear of the future, because they didn't really believe they could defeat their enemies in Canaan and claim the land. Ten of the twelve spies who surveyed the land said that, when they saw the "giants" inhabiting the area, they themselves looked like grasshoppers. They were walking by sight, not by faith, and had forgotten the promises of God.

In other words, they had hardened their hearts, and a hard heart usually leads to a rebellious heart. The Israelites had seen in Egypt what God could do, and yet they refused to trust Him and obey His word. When we deliberately ignore God's demonstrations of love and power and willfully go our own way, we are tempting God and asking Him to discipline us.

Five familiar words tell us how to avoid that repulsive sin and trustfully live in the present tense day by day, with and for our Lord Jesus Christ.

Excitement

When we live in the present tense, we live by faith and are able to welcome each day from God's hand, knowing that He always plans the best for us. Whether we wake up at home, in a motel, or in a hospital bed, we say confidently by faith, "This is the day the LORD has made; we will rejoice and be glad in it" (Ps. 118:24 NKJV). Our emphasis is on "the life I now live" (Gal. 2:20), the life of "good works, which God prepared in advance for us to do" (Eph. 2:10). We know that the Lord has planned each new day for us and that each day is tailor-made to bring us just what we need to keep us growing and serving (Ps. 139:16). Each day is an appointment, not an accident; and when our desire is to glorify God, we see opportunities as well as obstacles.

When we lose the excitement of the Christian life, we also start losing the enjoyment of the Christian life and become lukewarm believers like the church in Laodicea (Rev. 3:14–22). Instead of eagerly expecting each new day to be an adventure in faith, we yawn and start searching for something more exciting to do. Our daily devotional life becomes bland and routine, the occasional problems that come along make us impatient and angry, and eventually, blessing is replaced by boredom. Instead of thanking our Father for the good things He sends daily, we complain about what He doesn't send.

A. W. Tozer wrote, "A dopey, blear-eyed generation seeks constantly for some new excitement powerful enough to bring a thrill to its worn-out and benumbed sensibilities."[1] Ouch! Once Lot had gotten a taste of the intoxicating life of Egypt, he got tired of Uncle Abraham's life of faith and started moving toward Sodom (Gen. 13). As a result, Lot lost everything he owned when Sodom was destroyed, and he ended up in a cave committing incest with his two unmarried daughters. Lot didn't end well.

If you knew that each day would bring you joy and wealth, your life would be marked by excitement and anticipation. But that is exactly what our heavenly Father promises us! "I rejoice in following your statutes as one rejoices in great riches," wrote the psalmist. "I rejoice in your promise like one who finds great spoil" (Ps. 119:14, 162). Life is short and the days move swiftly, so we can't afford to waste them. "Teach us to number our days, that we may gain a heart of wisdom" (90:12).

When we find ourselves yawning instead of yearning, the only remedy is to repent, confess our sins, open the Scriptures, and hear a reviving word from the Lord. "The law of the LORD is perfect, refreshing the soul" (Ps. 19:7). Lose the excitement of living by faith, a day at a time, and you will end up on a costly detour.

Appointment

"Do two walk together unless they have agreed to do so?" asked the prophet Amos (3:3). The New American Standard Bible reads, "Do two men walk together unless they have made an appointment?" Each of God's children must have an appointed time and place for meeting God daily and devoting themselves to worship, prayer, and meditation in the Word. God made me to be a morning person, and I get my best work done between 5:30 a.m. and 3:00 p.m., but not everybody is made that way. I have successful friends who don't really begin working until about 8:00 in the evening and keep going until 3:00 a.m. The important thing is that *each day we give our very best time to the Lord.* Call it what you will—your quiet time, your prayer time, the upward look, daily devotions—it must be an uninterrupted time of fellowship with God in prayer and the Word, a time that sends us into our daily tasks prepared in spirit and happy with the will of God. *The most important part of our lives is the part that only God sees.* Problems must be solved privately in the prayer closet before they can be tackled publicly. Moses, Aaron, and Hur interceding on the mountain enabled Joshua and his army to win as they fought the Amalekites down below (Ex. 17:8–15).

We must begin our appointment with personal worship, thanking the Father for providentially giving us a new day, thanking the Son for dying for us and promising His presence with us, and thanking the Holy Spirit for the power and wisdom He will give as we face the demands and dangers of life. I like to read a hymn of praise to the Lord that expresses my gratitude far better than I can in my own words, although I believe the Father rejoices to hear His children's unrefined words of praise.

Finally, we must take time to be holy. Rushing through worship, prayer, and meditation means grieving the Lord. "What! Could you not watch with Me one hour?" (Matt. 26:40 NKJV). Quickly reading a few Bible verses, scanning a paragraph or two of devotional thoughts, and then rushing off to our daily duties means robbing ourselves of "hearing" God's voice, meditating on what He says, and "digesting" the truth within our hearts. Our daily devotional time is not a marathon in which we try to read a given number of verses each day. There are times when I find myself lingering over one verse and discovering truths in it I never saw before. God's Word is our food (4:4) and we must chew it carefully, not gulp it down.

Let's move to that topic now.

Enlightenment

"Your word is a lamp to my feet and a light for my path.... The unfolding of your words gives light; it gives understanding to the

simple" (Ps. 119:105, 130). The word translated "unfolding" is
literally "opening" and can be translated "doorway." Since ancient
houses did not have windows, when the door was opened, the sunlight would burst into the room. A closed Bible gives no light, and a
closed heart receives no light. (See Luke 24:32.) The word translated
"simple" could refer to a naive person who is easily deceived, but
here it describes a person who has not been formally taught in a
classroom, what Acts 4:13 calls an unschooled and ordinary person.

The Bible is an ancient book, yet it is always contemporary and
helps us live in the present tense. The Holy Spirit reveals Jesus to
us on its pages and gives us the truth we need for each day. "All
Scripture is God-breathed and is useful for teaching, rebuking, cor-
recting and training in righteousness, so that all God's people may be
thoroughly equipped for every good work" (2 Tim. 3:16–17). The
Bible belongs to all of God's people, not just the seminary gradu-
ates or the highly intelligent. The writers, "though human, spoke
from God as they were carried along by the Holy Spirit" (2 Peter
1:21). The Holy Spirit not only inspired God's Word, but He also
instructs us in God's Word. "But when he, the Spirit of truth, comes,
he will guide you into all the truth," said Jesus. "He will glorify me
because it is from me that he will receive what he will make known
to you" (John 16:13–14). The Spirit reveals Jesus in the Word just as
Jesus showed Himself in the Word to the Emmaus disciples (Luke
24:25–27).

We all know that we can see Jesus in the types and prophecies of
the Bible, but we can also see Him in the events (1 Cor. 10:1–13),
the people, and the promises (2 Cor. 1:18–22). Before G. Campbell
Morgan gave his exposition each Friday evening at the Westminster

Chapel Bible School in London, he had the congregation stand and sing the beautiful song "Break Thou the Bread of Life." I especially appreciate the stanza that says, "Beyond the sacred page / I seek Thee, Lord / My spirit pants for Thee, O Living Word." To read the Bible and not see Jesus is to miss the greatest blessing of all.

Remember, the Holy Spirit was present when the events took place and the words were spoken that are recorded in Scripture, beginning with creation (Gen. 1:1–2) and ending with God's last invitation and the apostle's last prayer (Rev. 22:17–21). The Spirit is an eyewitness who can help us see and understand the truth God wants us to live.

When God gave us the gift of His Son, He gave us His very best *and in Him everything we will ever need to live a successful Christian life!* "For no matter how many promises God has made, they are 'Yes' in Christ. And so through him the 'Amen' is spoken by us to the glory of God" (2 Cor. 1:20). We live by promises, not by explanations; and when through the Spirit we claim a promise and say "Amen—so be it," God fulfills the promise in Jesus Christ!

I like to recall the promises my wife and I have claimed and that the Lord has fulfilled in our family and our various ministries. Each promise had been in the Bible for centuries, but the Holy Spirit pointed them out to us just when we needed them most. We didn't consult a concordance or turn the pages of the Bible searching for them. In the course of our daily Bible reading, these promises jumped right off the page and shouted, "Trust me!" In Jesus Christ, God has "given us everything we need for a godly life" (2 Peter 1:3), and the keys that open this rich treasury are the unfailing promises of God. God has already said "Yes" in His Son,

and we should say a believing "Amen" to claim God's promise. If
we do, one day that promise will be fulfilled in the way that glorifies God the most.

Encouragement

The Christian life is not a solo enterprise, and the self-confident
believer who tries to make it that will be disappointed. After all,
Christians belong to the same spiritual body and are sheep in the
same flock, soldiers in the same army, and children in the same family, to name but a few of the many images of the church in Scripture.
These images indicate clearly that we belong to each other, we affect
each other, and we need each other. Frequently you find the phrase
one another in the New Testament—love one another, forgive one
another, edify one another, be kind to one another—and *one another*
speaks of mutual concern and care.

Hebrews 3:13 admonishes us, "But encourage one another daily,
as long as it is called 'Today,' so that none of you may be hardened
by sin's deceitfulness." In the early days of the church, the believers
daily met in the temple courts, daily provided food for the widows,
and daily led others to Christ (Acts 2:46–47; 6:1); so they had daily
opportunities to encourage each other. Hebrews 10:25 commands
believers to encourage each other to attend the regular meetings of
the church where they could give and receive even more encouragement. Some Christians have a special gift of encouragement and
must not hesitate to use it (Rom. 12:6, 8).

The Scottish preacher and writer John Watson, who wrote under
the name Ian Maclaren, used to say, "Be kind, for everyone you

meet is fighting a battle." I wrote that quotation in the front of my Bible and often looked at it before I stepped into the pulpit. There are many causes of discouragement in these difficult days, and our preaching, teaching, and counseling must assist people to rise above discouragement and believe the promises of God. Believers who are living in the present tense should be sensitive to the needs of others and take time to show concern, to listen, and to encourage.

Enablement

The Lord wants to use these powerful I AM statements in and through our lives, both to help us personally and enable us to help others.

Distributors. For example, Jesus is the bread of life (John 6:35), and we feed on Him through the Word (vv. 68–69). But He feeds us that we might in turn feed others. We are not only to *receive* a blessing but also to *be* a blessing (Gen. 12:2; Ps. 1:3). Like the servants at the wedding (John 2:1–10) and the apostles in John 6, *we are distributors, not manufacturers!* We say with Peter, "Silver or gold I do not have, but what I do have I give you" (Acts 3:6). We cannot give others what we don't have ourselves, and the Lord is willing and able to fill our hearts and hands so we may feed others. Don't try to manufacture blessings. Jesus has cornered the market.

Often in my ministry of preaching, teaching, and writing, I have felt like the man in the parable who had no bread to give his unexpected visitor and had to beg bread from a neighbor (Luke 11:5–8). *The Lord has always provided, sometimes at the last minute!* All it takes is a wedding, a funeral, and a church member dying in the hospital, and the study hours evaporate; but God has never failed me. Daily

I have asked Him to feed me from His Word, and there has always been bread in the cupboard.

Light bearers. Jesus is the light of the world (John 8:12), and as we follow Him, *we become lights to help others see their way.* The unconverted people in this world are walking in darkness and, sad to say, so are too many professed Christians (1 John 1:5–10). And when the crisis comes, they look to us for light. "I am sending you to them to open their eyes and turn them from darkness to light" (Acts 26:17–18). "You are the light of the world" (Matt. 5:14).

Followers. Jesus is the good shepherd, and as His obedient sheep, we feed in green pastures and are refreshed by the quiet waters (Ps. 23:2). He gives us provision ("I lack nothing," v. 1) and protection ("I will fear no evil," v. 4), so we have all that we need. Not only do we bring joy to His heart, but we are also good examples for the other sheep to imitate. No matter how much training and experience we have had, in order to be effective leaders, we must first be obedient followers.

Wonders. Jesus is the resurrection and the life (John 11:25–26), and we who have trusted Him have been raised from spiritual death and given everlasting life (Eph. 2:1–10). *We are living miracles!* The people who attended the funeral of Lazarus hurried to his home in Bethany four days later to see him alive! Lazarus could say with the psalmist, "I have become a marvel to many" (Ps. 71:7 NASB). There was not one recorded word of Lazarus the people could reference. They simply had to look at him, and they trusted Jesus (John 12:9–11)! I want my Lord to help me "live a new life" (Rom. 6:4) so that I can be a walking miracle and point others to the Savior. Let's keep our lives on a miracle basis to the glory of God.

Travelers. Jesus is the way and because we have trusted Him, our assured destination is the Father's house (John 14:6). We are on the right way because we have believed the truth and received the life (Matt. 7:13–14). To believe the truth but not walk in the way is to miss the life. They go together. Those who don't believe the truth as it is in Jesus do not have the life that Jesus gives, and they would be miserable in the Father's house. The popular philosophy today is that there are no absolutes and that Christians are not politically correct to say that faith in Jesus is the only way to be saved. But Jesus is *the* way and not one of many ways. As we obediently continue our pilgrimage on the way, we discover more truth and enjoy more of the abundant life.

Fruit bearers. Abiding as branches in Jesus, the vine, is the only way to enjoy a life of fruitfulness and usefulness (John 15:1–17). This means experiencing painful pruning so that we might be able to bear more and better fruit, but this is what glorifies our Lord. And we must keep in mind that *the branches do not eat the fruit; they share it with others.* Age, experience, and talent have very little to do with this remarkable fruit bearing; the secret is the faith, love, and obedience that enable us to abide in Christ. Around the time of my eightieth birthday, I was praying about my ministry and the painful limitations age can bring, and the Lord gave me assurance from Psalm 92:14: "They will still bear fruit in old age, they will stay fresh and green." What a birthday gift!

Paul wrote, "But by the grace of God I am what I am" (1 Cor. 15:10).

If you and I want that same kind of testimony, we must live in the present tense, abiding in Jesus Christ, who says, "I AM."

.

Notes

Chapter 1

1. Raymond W. Albright, *Focus on Infinity: A Life of Phillips Brooks* (New York: Macmillan, 1961), 349.

2. Theodore H. Epp, *Moses, Vol. 1* (Lincoln, NE: Back to the Bible, 1975), 86.

Chapter 4

1. Jaroslav Pelikan, *The Vindication of Tradition* (New Haven: Yale University Press, 1984), 65–66.

2. Dr. and Mrs. Howard Taylor, *The Biography of James Hudson Taylor* (London: China Inland Mission, 1965), 162–63.

Chapter 5

1. The NIV translates the word *thura* as "gate," but the more familiar word is "door," used by the KJV, NKJV, NEB, ESV, RSV, and NASB.

2. The Hebrew word *Hanukkah* means "dedication."

3. A ninth candle stands in the middle of the menorah. It is used to light the other eight.

Chapter 8

1. But see Ex. 4:22; Deut. 32:6; Isa. 63:16; 64:8; Jer. 3:4, 19; Mal. 1:6; 2:10.

2. For more about God's Word as food, see Matt. 4:4; 1 Peter 2:2; 1 Cor. 3:1–4; Heb. 5:11–14; Job 23:12; Jer. 15:16. Please read these verses.

3. Material in this section is adapted from my book on the parable of the Prodigal Son, *Another Chance at Life,* and is used by permission of the publishers, Christian Literature Crusade (2009).

Chapter 9

1. For those who did not study chemistry 101, H_2O is water and H_2SO_4 is sulfuric acid.

Chapter 11

1. In 1 Timothy 1:15–16, Paul says that his conversion experience was "an example for those who would believe in him," and in 1 Corinthians 15:8 that he was "abnormally born." I have never met or heard of a Christian who saw Jesus in His glory and heard Him speak as Paul did. I think Paul was referring to his beloved fellow Jews who would one day see their Messiah and believe in Him (Zech. 12:10; Matt. 24:30–31). Paul was "born early" as an example of what would happen to the Jews at the return of Christ.

2. See Acts 13:47; 26:18, 23; Rom. 13:12; 1 Cor. 4:5; 2 Cor. 4:4–6; 6:14; 11:14; Eph. 1:18; 5:8–14; Phil. 2:15; Col. 1:12; 1 Thess. 5:5; 1 Tim. 6:16; 2 Tim. 1:10.

3. D. L. Moody, *Glad Tidings* (New York: E. B. Treat, 1876), 291–292.

4. James S. Stewart, *A Man in Christ* (New York: Harper Brothers, n.d.), 83.

5. James Stalker, *The Life of St. Paul* (Old Tappan, NJ: Fleming H. Revell, 1950), 31.

Chapter 12

1. A. W. Tozer, *Born After Midnight* (Harrisburg, PA: Christian Publications, 1959), 68.

BIBLE CREDITS

Explore the truth of Scripture with Dr. Wiersbe

Let one of the most respected Bible teachers of our time guide you verse by verse through the Bible with the "BE" series commentaries and Bible studies. These timeless books provide invaluable insight into the history, meaning, and context of virtually every book in the Bible.

The "BE" series . . .

For years pastors and lay leaders have embraced Warren W. Wiersbe's very accessible commentary of the Bible through the individual "BE" series. Through the work of David C. Cook Global Mission, the "BE" series is part of a library of books made available to indigenous Christian workers. These are men and women who are called by God to grow the kingdom through their work with the local church worldwide. Here are a few of their remarks as to how Dr. Wiersbe's writings have benefited their ministry.

"Most Christian books I see are priced too high for me . . .
I received a collection that included 12 Wiersbe
commentaries a few months ago and I have
read every one of them.
I use them for my personal devotions every day and they
are incredibly helpful for preparing sermons.
The contribution David C. Cook is making to the
church in India is amazing."

—Pastor E. M. Abraham, Hyderabad, India